A Journalism Handbook
For Media Entrepreneurs

Compiled and edited by the Arkbound Foundation

A Journalism Handbook for Media Entrepreneurs

By the Arkbound Foundation

© 2017 Arkbound Foundation

ISBN 9781912092635

First published in 2018 by the Arkbound Foundation
Cover image and illustrations by Lucy McArthur 2017

■ ■

The Arkbound Foundation is an independent UK charity that aims to improve access to literature and journalism, boosting the diversity of both. We fully embrace sustainability and environmental protection, using material that is renewable, recyclable or sourced from sustainable forest.

Arkbound Foundation
Backfields House
Upper York Street
Bristol BS2 8QJ

www.arkfound.org

A Journalism Handbook
For Media Entrepreneurs

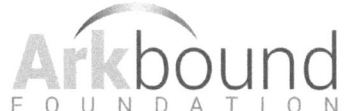

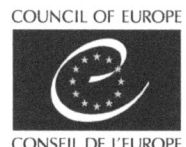

COUNCIL OF EUROPE

CONSEIL DE L'EUROPE

*'The Press is the best instrument for enlightening
the mind of man, and improving him as a rational,
moral and social being.'*
Thomas Jefferson

*'The people must know before they can act,
and there is no educator to compare with the press.'*
Ida Wells

'Queen backs Brexit.'
2017 UK Tabloid newspaper
headline claim (since proven false)

Acknowledgments

This book is based upon two earlier journalism handbooks written by Media in Cooperation & Transition (MICT), an organisation dedicated to creating an accessible and informative global media ecosystem. Without their prior work and assistance, it would not have been possible to create.

We are also grateful for the research, guidance, feedback and support given by Tassos Morfis, Anna Frenyo, Diane Kemp and Kathryn Geels.

Funding for this publication was generously given by the Alexander Mosley Charitable Foundation and the Council of Europe.

Contents

Contents 8

Foreword 12

JOURNALISM ESSENTIALS 16

Doing Due Diligence in Journalism 16

Choosing the Subject 18

Finding Story Ideas 20

Mind Mapping: Finding Fresh Angles.................22

Community Journalism Topics 23

Research...24

Story-telling 27

Working in Places of Conflict 29

The News Story...32

The News Feature...34

The Analysis...36

The Editorial 38

The Profile..40

The Feature Story 42

The Interview..44

The Story Proposal 47

ONLINE JOURNALISM 50

Writing for the Internet.......................................50

Mobile Photography –Taking Quality Images 52

Video Production with Smart Phones..................55

Radio Production with Smart Phones 58

The Use of Social Media 60

Social Media on the Internet 62

A Web of Change 65

Tips for Boosting Engagement Online 68

COMMUNITY ENGAGEMENT FOR HYPERLOCALS **70**

Questions for deciding who your target audience are 70

Social media 71

Community Engagement 72

SOURCES OF REVENUE FOR MEDIA OUTLETS **77**

Advertising **77**

Considerations for Advertisers 81

Closing an Advertising Deal 84

Advertorials **88**

Listings and Directories **89**

Membership Models **90**

Podcasts **91**

Crowdfunding **92**

Grant Funding **93**

Copy Sales **94**

Donations **95**

Promotional Services **97**

Events and Workshops **98**

Publishing Services **99**

Statutory Notices **100**

Sponsorship **101**

Selling Content **103**

Special Merchandise..104

Collaboration 105

RESOURCES..107

News Sites (National and International)..........................107

Key Resources 109

Freedom of Information 110

Photography sites and image formatting 111

Search Engine Optimisation 111

TOR...112

Further Reading 113

APPENDIX A: The Code of Conduct for Journalists...............114

APPENDIX B: Other Ways to Make Money with Journalism ..116

About the Arkbound Foundation 121

Foreword

The press has the power to educate and inspire; to inform and enlighten – generally, to form a key component of a healthy, democratic society. The invention of the printing press was one of the driving factors of the Renaissance, ushering into a period of rapid progression in science, culture and politics. More recently, the internet has allowed a globalized exchange of ideas and open platform of information to be accessed by all. We truly do live in an 'age of information', yet there needs to be a way for people to filter through this virtual cacophony and select things that are accurate, interesting and relevant. Here lies one of the central challenges for any media outlet, but it is not the only one.

Recent times have demonstrated how the press can be used for a tool for bad, as well as good. If you were to glance upon three of the largest tabloid's headlands, would you find the stories to be enlightening, educating, informative and inspirational? More likely they are written to play upon the reader's bias; even to mislead and manipulate public opinion in favor of the proprietor's interests. Over 70% of newspaper circulation in the UK is controlled by just three corporations, and these three have close connections to some of the country's wealthiest and powerful people. Owning a media outlet that can influence and mold national opinion is, in itself, an exercise of great power. And where regulation of press coverage is inconsistent and lax, there is a danger not just of people being misled but of democracy being undermined.

In some respects, poor journalistic practice in the mainstream print media has been an ingredient for its own demise. Since 1999, revenue for printed newspapers – both regionally and nationally – has been declining. Part of this can be attributed to the rise of digital media, but it is also no coincidence why there has been a corresponding fall in how many people trust newspaper: a survey in 2016 by Ofcom revealed that print media is the last place where people get their news from. Trust in newspapers is at an all-time low.

The failure of mainstream print media opens up opportunities. People who have traditionally been excluded from the industry now have the capacity to create and grow their own media outlets. It is no easy task, but there remains a persistent demand for quality and engaging publications that follow innovative models. Even for print media, a study by NESTA in 2016 has shown a *rise* in so-called 'hyperlocal' and niche publications, which engage smaller geographic areas or interests. Moreover, more established media have been finding ways to make income from such things as introducing special 'membership' schemes, raising money through crowdfunding, and providing special services.

This handbook aims to give an introduction to entrepreneurial journalism, so that you can learn the key skills to report and create good content, whilst upholding high standards. Learning these skills is essential to both starting a new media outlet or joining an existing one. It also provides a comprehensive look at the many different ways to make a media outlet financially sustainable, drawing upon real case studies and proven examples from across the world.

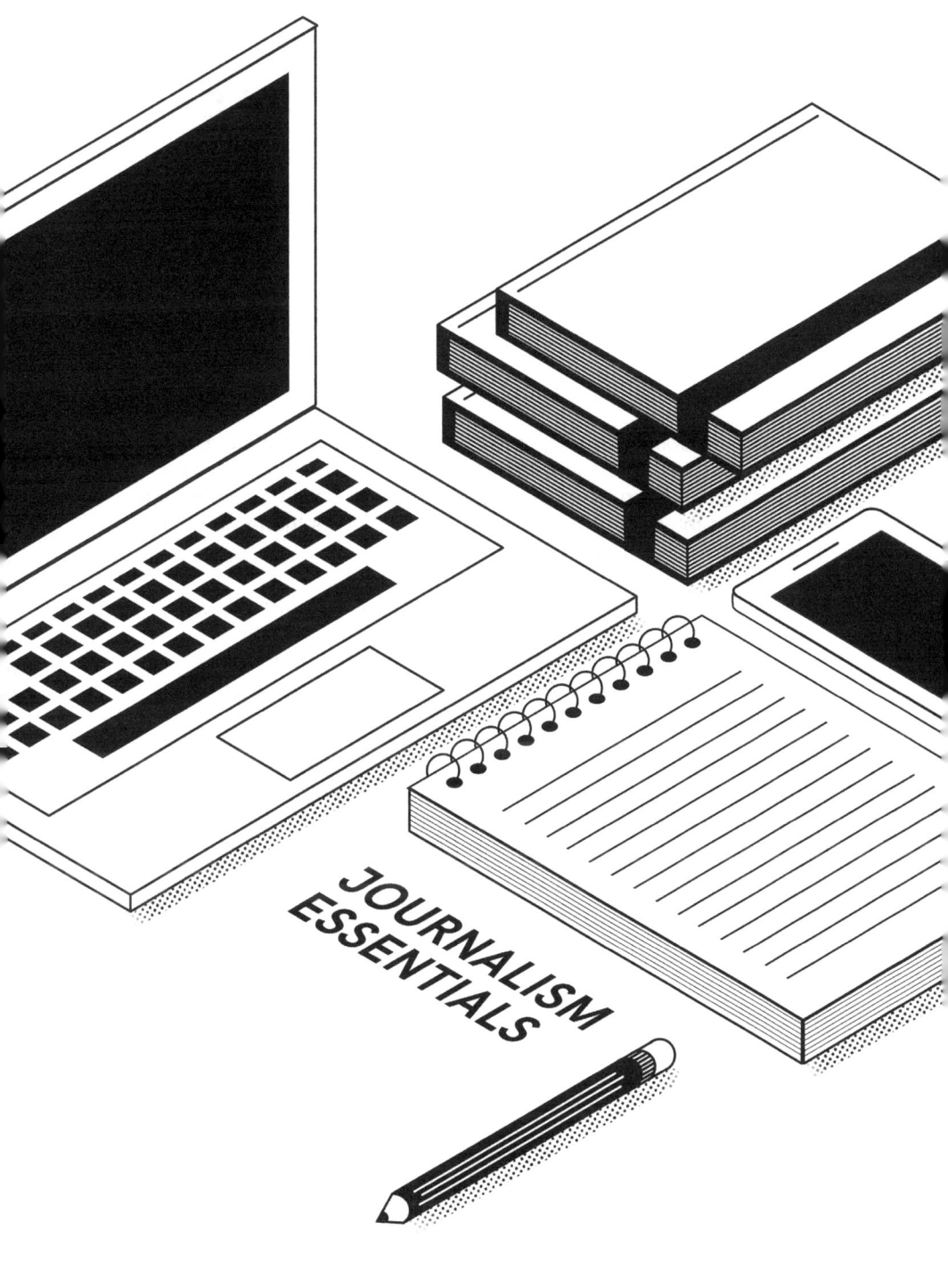

JOURNALISM ESSENTIALS

* * *

Doing Due Diligence in Journalism

The phrase "doing due diligence" means that all possible steps have been taken to avoid illegal activities or harming others. This means that the journalist has done all that is possible to ensure the information they are presenting is accurate, and is therefore acting in a professional and ethical manner.

The substance of the journalist's work should be informative, well researched and honest. It should also provide a balanced perspective and be supported by facts, sources and quotes. A crucial point to bear in mind is that the main facts in all journalistic work must be supported by more than one source.

In the event that reports or observations are not backed up by more than one source, or not supported by trustworthy sources, this must be made clear in the piece. Moreover, a journalist's work should not be influenced by their own private interests or others' agendas.

A journalist must protect sources, especially if the source has provided information that potentially harms them either physically or psychologically. If the source asks to remain anonymous, the journalist should not retract upon this unless further consultation with the source results in a different agreement.

The content of a journalist's work should not deliberately include bias. When the subject is likely to cause a dispute, then the journalist must ensure that the views of all sides involved in the conflict are represented fairly and accurately.

Journalists should use only relevant and important information in their stories. If one has included irrelevant points, one should protect the source's privacy. Journalists do not work "under cover," but should name the organisation they are employed by, the angle of the story, and the aim of the interview.

Finally, a journalist should aim to create original work and therefore should avoid copying other research, sources or documents word for word.

CHECKLIST

i. Is the work balanced? Are all sides fairly and evenly represented?

ii. Could some of the content arouse any conflicts or cause bias?

iii. Does some of the content lead to misinterpretation or has it been taken out of context?

iv. Is there content irrelevant to the topic?

v. Have the sources of the key points in the work been credited?

vi. Has the journalist been an observer and so maintained a professional detachment?

vii. Have personal interests or other agendas been averted?

viii. Throughout the piece, has the journalist protected their sources?

ix. Have the audience been given a credible reason of why the source is anonymous?

x. Was the journalist clear who they were while gaining information?

Choosing the Subject

The subject should be relevant to the community the journalist is working in. This could involve politics, economics, or social and cultural events that affect the community either locally, nationally, or even internationally.

Of most interest is new developments within a broad subject category, such as "education". The latest news for this category could include budget cuts for schools on the national level. At the local level, it may cover the opening of a new school in that area.

The topic being presented should reach the public at the right time and place, and can be influenced by the form of media being used.

Different types of media cover the news differently; broadcast media, for example, requires pictures, whilst radio media requires audio interviews. With a magazine, developments may be needed since the material is published at a later date.

The audience must also be considered. For example, the number of consumers of the information alters: the national evening news is watched by millions of people and so will cover developments differently from the community newspaper, which will usually only be read by several thousand people.

When choosing which developments within a subject category to cover, it is important to consider the medium the piece is for.

CHECKLIST

i.   Is the intelligence on the subject the most recent?

ii.   Does the subject have political, social, economic or cultural relevance?

iii.   Is the topic important to the local or national consumer?

iv.   Has the topic been covered on the right media platform?

v.   Is the information available to be published at the correct time in the right place?

vi.   How balanced is the reporting?

vii.   Are there to be further developments?

Finding Story Ideas

Many story ideas come from current events, such as parliamentary votes, cultural events, and disasters. Journalists need to research these events and present them to the public in an informative and appropriate manner.

As well as current events, a big aspect of a journalist's job is to find new stories and ideas. They can create new angles on topics that might not be in the public eye.

In order to do this, a journalist should keep up-to-date with all events going on around them across cultural, social, and political areas, questioning anything that happens.

A journalist should keep a diary of official dates, and be aware of what happens on those dates, whether or not it is a topic of their present work.

Create a 'contacts book' by finding, making and recording contacts that will provide you with new and helpful information either in present or future stories.

Journalists should keep aware of stories across all other types of media, as sometimes there are story opportunities created, or questions that need to be followed up or answered.

You should listen carefully to what people are thinking and talking about. If you find out what moves them, what motivates them and what they may be planning, there could be a story.

Maintaining and updating an understanding of people's opinions towards various situations allows you to get a good sense of public sentiment regarding different topics.

Cultivate a sense of curiosity at all times. When you have questions about a topic and want to know more, a journalist always follows up in case there is a story there.

CHECKLIST

How to find different story ideas

i. In press releases and on the websites of political parties, and organisations.

ii. At press conferences or meetings.

iii. At trade fairs.

iv. In my contacts book.

v. Online.

vi. In your daily life.

Mind Mapping: Finding Fresh Angles

New topics are generally the most interesting. So with topics that have been reported on numerous times in the past it can be difficult to find a new angle to engage your audience. Examples of subjects could include unemployment, the energy crisis, or the homeless.

Dates are also difficult to find a new angle for. Anniversaries that come around each year, like Christmas or national celebrations are two instances.

Mind mapping can aid journalists and editors in thinking of something new and more interesting for the public on an already well-reported subject.

Mind mapping helps to reveal new viewpoints and alternative perspectives on a particular topic.
Specifically, mind mapping comes up with associations that could make an interesting story. It provides a way for the journalist to consider everything associated with certain key words or phrases.

Through taking the time to focus on a subject, such as an interesting protagonist, the journalist will be able to come up with new ideas surrounding that topic, for example, the environment in which the protagonist is employed.

Community Journalism Topics

Subjects that interest people tend to be those that relate to their everyday lives. Broader topics, therefore, need to be made relevant and interesting for a local audience when broadcasting for community media forms.

Most topics with global or national relevance will have an aspect important to the local community. For example, a new tax law being passed at a national level can create a story for a local journalist exploring how this affects the community.

In the case of a national medical emergency like a flu epidemic, a journalist can find out how local doctors and hospitals plan to deal with it.

If a national football match is to be played, a story focusing on a local club which trains young players in order to help them break into premiership teams might be interesting for the local community.

CHECKLIST

i.   Does the national or global news have an effect on the local people?

ii.   Are there expert community members who are available to address this topic?

iii. Could I use global or national news to start a local discussion?

Research

Research enables journalists to determine whether information they have gathered is true and accurate. It assists the journalist in making an unbiased observation, and helps them to report the complete story.

As a result, research could give both the journalist and their audience access to information that may not be currently available to the public.

Research is vital, as journalists need to be certain they have got all the information from all angles so as to carefully and accurately fulfill their professional duties.

By researching every aspect of a subject, the journalist reaches their conclusions independently, and so avoids aligning their views with others' agendas.

Research needs to be supported by the media in which the reports appear, and good media organisations should both support and develop research.

When new information arrives, prior to researching, check:

1. Whether the information is important enough to require further research.

2. If the source can be considered trustworthy. How did the source gain their information - was it first or second-hand, online, elsewhere?

3. If the information is bias because of a source. Does the source have credibility? How is the source related to the topic?

Fact-checking considerations:

1. Is this information genuine and correct? Is all of the information surrounding the story there?

2. Is the information coherent?

3. Is there a clear storyline, or causality?

4. Does this information appear to be true?

The steps involved in researching:

1. **Gather information:** anything you can find that has been published on the topic.

2. **Investigate sources:** conduct interviews with witnesses, victims, experts and critics. Try to speak to people in order of neutrality. For example, the even-minded experts, then those with political agendas, and finally more biased individuals like critics and victims.

3. **Personal reflection:** your personal experiences could be helpful. They also allow you to add colour to the piece.

CHECKLIST

i. What is the relevance of the new information? Are the sources reputable? How factual, true and coherent is the information?

ii. Does this information merit further investigation?

iii. Have the guidelines towards researching been followed as closely as possible?

iv. Has enough research been done? Can you carry out an effective interview with the information already gathered?

v. Have you been able to interview all relevant individuals?

vi. Have the neutral interviewees been spoken with first?

vii. Are all of the sources trustworthy and accurate?

viii. Have two sources confirmed the most important information? Has the journalist maintained a professional distance?

ix. Could the information or story be improved by the journalist's own experiences?

Story-telling

In journalism, storytelling presents information in a way that enables the audience to understand and remember it effectively. They do this best when stories are told in an engaging way and with good narration.

What is in stories that we enjoy?

- An introduction to a new, enthralling topic.
- People we can identify with.
- An ability to create an emotional response.
- A common theme, topic or idea.
- Are gripping all the way through.
- Are told well.

What does a good story have?

- A clear focus.
- A protagonist.
- A setting.
- A common theme, a gripping introduction, some high points, and a satisfying ending.
- A clear evolution with well-timed drama.
- Descriptive and exciting language.
- A narrator who is present.

Storytelling occurs in which media formats?

Feature-style stories like portraits, features, and background features can occur in print, radio, TV, and online.

CHECKLIST

i.   What story am I to tell? Is there a focus point that could make the story more compelling?

ii. Could some characters make the story particularly good? Will my audience trust these people?

iii. Are there particular places that give my story more life?

iv. How will I begin my story?

v.   How do I keep my audience's interest from faltering? Does some conflict appear? Which events, questions, or facts should I keep until the ending?

vi. What is the best structure for this story?

vii. Is the language in my story vibrant enough? Is the pace of my storytelling fast enough so people do not lose interested?

viii. Do I have a distinct voice so that my audience knows it is me?

Working in Places of Conflict

Some stories could be in places of conflict, crisis or turmoil and often these can arise in previously safe areas. Journalists may swiftly find themselves in situations that are dangerous – for example, in the middle of a riot, caught in-between two different sides, or covering serious criminal activity.

In such situations the journalist faces many threats: any equipment like cameras and microphones may be damaged or stolen; they may personally experience abuse or even physical attack.

No matter how important a story could be, a journalist's personal security must be a priority, as well as the security of all those involved in the journalistic work. It may sometimes be appropriate and necessary for a journalist to work in a place of conflict, but they must do so being mindful of all the risks. All possible steps to keep the journalist safe, and all those they are responsible for, should be taken.

CHECKLIST

i. You may need your identity documents if stopped by the police. Try to have a copy of your passport or driving license, together with your press card.

ii. Plan field reporting meticulously and after thorough research. Ensure no one is there for longer than necessary and that equipment is used efficiently.

iii. Keep your mobile on you and always have fully charged batteries in reserve, with mobile numbers carried separately on paper in the event that your mobile is lost.

iv. Ensure you do not use regular travelling routes or times.

v. Obey social, religious and cultural customs of the location.

vi. Clothing should enable you to be innocuous but not look military.

vii. All vehicles should be checked thoroughly prior to the trip for petrol, spare tyres and keys, plus a full battery.

viii. Prior to leaving, consider all possible scenarios and responses to them.

ix. Keep updating a home base and check in regularly with others. Avoid working by yourself.

x. Completing a first aid course is recommended by organisations like 'Reporters Without Borders'.

What to do if there are escalating demonstrations or protests:

i. In the event that tear gas is used, keep car windows closed. If you are outside the vehicle, keep your hands away from your eyes and do not go into the wind. Contact lenses and eye makeup can exacerbate the effects. First aid kits should include masks for use against tear gas.

ii. If the protest is pre-planned, check the route and surrounding area first to work out the location of the demonstrators and security forces, as well as to plan escape routes.

iii. Find out if the demonstrators will use weapons or projectiles. Consider the equipment security forces may be carrying: tear gas, rubber bullets, and water-cannons.

iv. Carry a small set of first aid equipment as well as a protective vest, a helmet, and a gas mask.

v. Never stand between the police and demonstrators with your back to one side or the other.

The News Story

A news story is a precise report about an event. Its main function is to inform. Writer's opinions are not usually in new stories. The key qualities of a news story are accuracy, brevity, and clarity.

The construction of a news story

The most important information about the event is located at the beginning of the story. Some extra and important information then follows on in a logical sequence.

The least important information is kept until the end. If the story needs to be shortened the ending can then easily be modified without losing important details.

The information in a news story

A news story answers the five W's and one H:

- What?
- Who?
- Where?
- When?
- Why?
- How?

It may not always be possible to gain all of the answers from the same place and at the same time, but if any of the 5 questions are not answered then the news story will remain incomplete.

The length of a news story

News stories tend to be between 200 and 500 words long.

How the news story is written

The subject of the news story must be as precise as possible, with a mix of short and long sentences where appropriate. A news story should be direct and avoid being too complex or overly descriptive. The journalist should not include foreign words or abbreviations that may be unfamiliar to the audience.

CHECKLIST

i.   Is the news in the story up-to-date and does it inform the reader about anything new?

ii.   Is the most vital information at the beginning of the story?

iii.   Would the reader glean the point of the story from the first few sentences?

iv.   Are the five W's and one H answered?

v.   Could the reader understand the story without having to read any other articles?

vi.   Does the story inform the reader as to the relevance of all the people mentioned? Are contexts or abbreviations explained?

vii.   Is there any bias or inaccuracies in the story?

viii.   Does the story include any irrelevant details you need to cut?

ix.   Is the story a good length?

The News Feature

A news feature is based on a current event, but provides more detail than simple news stories. Whilst a news feature includes further information, it withholds judgments or comments.

The construction of a news feature

The most important and most up-to-date information will be found in the first paragraph. The news feature will ensure it answers the five W's at the top of the story. The rest of the news feature includes further detail on each of the five W's.

The information in a news feature

The news feature can include detailed facts such as dates and statistics, as well as a greater number of quotes and interviews than news stories.

Whilst the interviewees may make judgments and comments, the journalist may not. News features may also incorporate live action or eyewitness accounts, as well as information about the scene that the journalist experienced.

The length of a news feature

News features can be anywhere between 500 and 1,500 words long. Usually, they are shorter than more detailed features on less current topics, but longer than simple news reports.

How a news feature is written

Concise and objective language is key to a news feature. The story tends to be comprised of a combination of longer and shorter sentences and avoids being overly complex or descriptive. Again, the news feature avoids foreign words and abbreviations where possible.

CHECKLIST

i.   Is the information on the news feature as current as possible?

ii.   Does the news feature contain a new and relevant item for a reader?

iii.   Are the five W's and one H answered in the first few paragraphs?

iv.   Does the body of the story go into the five W's and the one H in more detail?

v.   Are the most important questions answered first?

vi.   Could the reader understand the story without having to read any other articles?

vii.   Does the story inform the reader of the relevance of all people mentioned? Are locations and abbreviations explained?

viii.   Is the story accurate and neutral?

The Analysis

An analysis aims to analyse and evaluate a new story. It differs from other kinds of feature stories in that, rather than exposing facts and investigating or telling a story, it aims mainly to explain.

In order to explain, a journalist may seek expert opinions and follow a specific line of argument.

However, this is not an editorial, a commentary, or pure opinion. The interviewees are free to make judgments and comment, but the journalist is not. Any analysis must be supported by research, objective facts and figures.

An analysis mentions the original news story upon which it is based. Any additional facts and opinions must be organised as they are in a news feature (See News Feature section).

The analysis often introduces new protagonists, interviewees or experts with particular connections to the topic.

A short analysis is often around 200 words long. A longer analysis could be as long as a smaller news feature, between 500 and 1,000 words.

Generally, the language used in an analysis is concise and neutral. Sometimes the language can be more relaxed, as in feature writing. The reader should be able to base their opinion on an analysis.

CHECKLIST

i.   Is the research organised in a way that the events appear to the reader in a new way?

ii.   Is the research organised in a logical manner?

iii.   Is all the relevant background information included in the analysis?

The Editorial

Opinions or viewpoints made by the author can be included in an editorial. The piece includes all of the information that resulted in the journalist reaching this opinion.

A commentary / editorial seeks to persuade the reader to agree with this opinion through the presentation of a well-explained and informed argument.

The construction of a commentary/editorial

Firstly, the reader must be informed by a commentator or editorialist about which issue is being discussed.

They must provide facts, information and arguments that led him or her to this point of view about the issue. The commentator or editorialist is the informant and must share the information he or she has with the reader.

Having done all this, the author will then draw their final conclusion. Generally, commentaries and editorials follow three steps:

1. What is this the topic of this commentary? This includes the 5 W's and one H from news reporting: where, what, who, when, why and how.

2. Why is the author making a critique? Why is the author supporting something? What formed the author's opinions? Does the author have any background information? Is the author an expert or an informed writer?
3. What is the conclusion? It could be anything from showing a different point-of-view, a problem's alternative solution, providing a light on continuing concerns, asking unresolved questions or making a strong condemnation.

How is a commentary / editorial written and laid-out?

Generally, an editorial is between 300 and 800 words long. An editorial should be relatively short.

To differentiate the editorial as an opinion, rather than fact, the layout should differ. This can be done through varying font, headlines, special pages, disclaimers or other signifiers.

The style of writing can go from ironic or humorous to polemical and combative. However, the style must cohere with the topic and argument. Readers would take an editorial less seriously, if the style does not suit the subject.

CHECKLIST

i. What point is the author trying to make? What conclusions do they come to?

ii. Does the commentary entail all the information that supports the author's conclusion?

iii. Is the topic of discussion clear to readers?

iv. Does the author use their argument and information to create a coherent conclusion?

v. Does the tone of the commentary suit the argument and topic the author has discussed?

The Profile

A profile is a description of a person or organisation. Writing a profile involves using many different skills in an attempt to create a lifelike image of the individual or person who is being profiled.

Readers are to draw their own conclusions from / make their own judgments about the profile based on the quotes and details that the writer has included.

A cinematic style of profiles includes "close-ups" and "wide angle shots". The "close-up" is used to present the reader with details of the profile's subject or scene. The "wide angle shot" is used to give the reader details about things like facts, history, backgrounds and some other information.

Both of the "shots" are used interchangeably. The profile should continuously maintain all the storytelling tension and interest.

There are three different types of profile:

1. A profile of a person

2. A profile of a city / place

3. A profile of an institution / organisation.

A writer should always try to emphasise and detail the human aspects in a profile, even if that profile is not about an individual person. This avoids the profile becoming dull.

Profiles should generally be about 800-1,000 words long.

A profile can sometimes be shortened to five hundred words, but in this case it would contain more straightforward information about the subject. Shorter profiles are generally used when the subject is currently in the news and time is restricted in terms of access to research or interviews.

The guidelines for the language used in profiles can be fairly broad. They are:

- Descriptive language that engages all five of the reader's senses should be used
- A profile should show, not tell.
- The writer should try and write the profile in a creative and unique way.
- The details included in the profile should always be consistent with, or important to, the story being told.

CHECKLIST

i. Should the profile be answering a specific or important question about the subject?

ii. Which details about the subject are the most profound?

iii. Could the profile include the opinions of others, for example friends, enemies or colleagues?

iv. Has the writer used the "close-up" and "wide angle" techniques efficiently?

v. Is the storytelling tension maintained throughout the profile?

The Feature Story

Feature stories are longer and are generally about topics including politics, culture and society, sport or business. A feature differs from a commentary because it informs the reader about the subject; features can be just as lively and compelling however, if they're written in such a way.

Similar to a commentary, readers are expected to draw their own conclusions from a feature based on quotes and information the writer has chosen to include, and a feature is expected to show rather than tell.

Features can be written in a variety of ways. They quite often weave factual information and colourful real life scenes together, using the facts to accompany and explain the scenes.

The most interesting facts and scenes should be evenly spread out over the course of the feature. Just like a commentary, a feature cannot be shortened from the bottom of a story.

There are many different types of feature story. They can include things like eye-witness accounts describing what it was like to be at a particular event or scene. They can also be investigative, using a huge amount of research and analysis, as well as interviews, to convey information about a subject.

Here are some examples of a feature story:

- News backgrounders or analysis
- Trend or cultural features
- Eyewitness accounts
- Investigative features
- Literary features
- Profiles

In many circumstances, the differing styles of feature story will intersect. A news feature will often use the same information as a profile, particularly if the subject is one particular individual.

Profiles also often use the same information as features, for instance a description of the subject's meeting with the journalist.

The best features usually have a minimum word count of 1,000. They can be far longer though; magazines will often publish anything between 4,000 and 10,000 words.

Like a commentary, there are no strict rules about the language one should use when writing a feature. However, the language should be compelling and creative and should bring across a style unique to both the writer and the story.

CHECKLIST

i.   Is there a particular location which sets the scene for this story?

ii.   Is the subject of the story on one individual or protagonist?

iii.   If there is more than one protagonist, are their different perspectives well portrayed? Are their stories different enough to create a wholesome picture of what is happening?

iv.   Is there a consistent theme that runs throughout the whole story?

v.   Do the facts and scenes connect together logically?

vi.   Does the beginning of the feature grab the reader's attention straight away? Does the feature conclude in a rounded way, while adhering to the piece's central theme?

The Interview

An interview piece will convey the meeting of a journalist and a specific subject, or interviewee, whose opinions and career are related to a topic that is of interest to readers.

In an interview, the journalist acts on behalf of the reader, asking questions about the subject's life, opinions or career. The journalist's own opinions are rarely relevant during the interview.

There are several different kinds of interviews. They can be defined as the following:

- Interviews on a certain topic or event: individuals or experts are asked to provide information on that event.
- Interviews for opinions and analysis: Experts or individuals provide opinions on, or analysis of certain topics or events. They then may be scrutinised by the interviewer based on these opinions or analyses.
- Interviews on a more personal basis: The interviewer will ask an individual question based on who they are. This could relate to their talents, current affairs or various other things.

It is quite often the case that the boundaries between the various interview formats are blurred.
Interviewers should always avoid asking questions that can result in "yes" or "no" answers. They should also avoid questions which might give the interviewee cause to stumble over their words or blunder.
The questions should indulge the interest of the reader, and the interviewer should also attempt to remain critical; questions that the subject might enjoy being asked should be avoided.

Interviews are usually begun by an introductory paragraph that relays who the interviewee is and current details about any major topic that will be discussed in the interview. The distinct focus of the interview should be laid out in these introductory paragraphs.

The Interview should maintain the reader's interest until the end, and fluidity is important – the questions and answers should relate to each other profoundly.

A good interviewer will respond to what the interviewee says and could improvise questions based upon this. Generally, questions shouldn't be longer than 3-4 lines and answers should not exceed 10-15 lines.

The language used in an interview depends on the context of the interview. The interview could either be conducted in a colloquial, conversational manner or in a completely professional style.

Any words or language that might be understood by experts needs to be "translated" so that every day people will also understand. Technical terms and abbreviations must be explained.

One should try and keep as much of the interviewee's character and personality in the interview as possible.

CHECKLIST

i. Is an interview the correct format for the topic being discussed? In a profile or a feature, for example, information, journalistic observations and the interviewee's perspective could be used.

ii. Does the reader have a clear understanding of who the interviewee is and why they're being interviewed?

iii. Does the reader have a clear understanding of why certain questions are being asked as the interview progresses? Do the answers adequately respond to the questions?

iv. Have things like jargon, technical language and expert opinions been translated so the reader can understand them?

v. Has any unnecessary information and generally unhelpful chatter been removed from the finished version of the interview?

vi. Were all the questions answered that could have been of particular importance to the readers?

vii. Is the time and authorisation of the interview apparent?

The Story Proposal

The story proposal is necessary because it is vital that the journalist and the editor communicate; it determines whether the editor will want the journalist to work on the story.

The story proposal allows the journalist to clarify his or her idea and outline exactly what they are trying to achieve and how they are going to achieve it.

Every story needs to have a specific angle or focus. The angle of a story will force the journalist to think about the best way to approach a topic and consider why the reader should care about the story. It will be the angle or focus which defines this. The rest of the story will develop naturally out of this starting point.

For example:

- The major topic: Agriculture
- The angle/ focus: A small business trying to grow new kinds of vegetables.
- The story: A small agricultural business is attempting to breed new varieties of broccoli. This broccoli can feed six families. The journalist could try getting in touch with the business owners, people who have eaten the broccoli, store owners that sell the broccoli and maybe some experts in the field of agriculture and nutrition.

CHECKLIST

The best story proposals are generally written over the course of several short, succinct paragraphs that will explain the focus of the story, how it will be researched and the point it is trying to convey. Generally, story proposals should include the following:

i.   A story explanation in 3-4 sentences.

ii.   Discuss whether the topic has been covered before, and how.

iii.   How is the journalist's story new and different?

iv.   How will the journalist make this story interesting to readers?

v.   What research will be done and who is the interviewee?

vi.   What sort of format is the angle of the story best suited to?

vii.   How long will the story take to complete, including all the research and writing that the journalist will do?

viii.   What is the minimum word count that will best convey everything that the journalist is trying to put across with their story?

ix.   Will the journalist need the editor's support at all? This could include things like a commissioning letter or letters of recommendation.

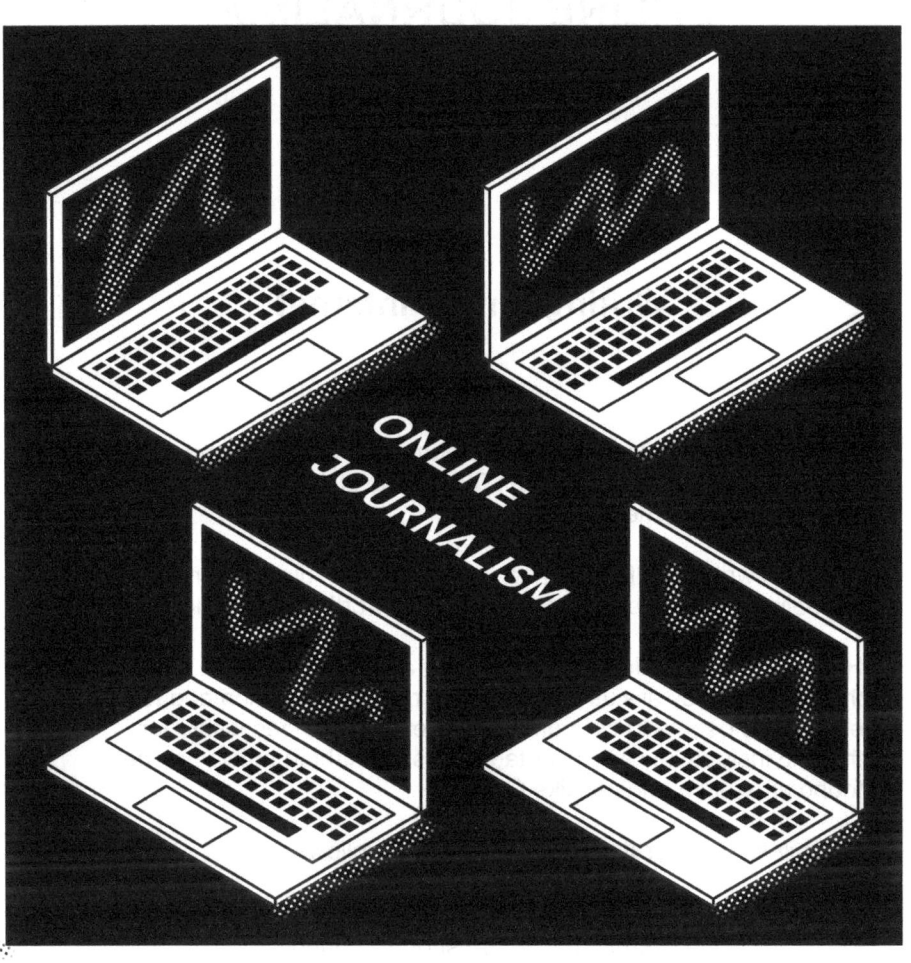

ONLINE JOURNALISM

* * *

Writing for the Internet

In the age of the Internet, every differing kind of writing and journalism can be found online. There is no style of writing that is distinct to the internet.

Although writing on the Internet adheres to the rules general to journalism, there are several other things worth considering.

Headlines, subheads and teasers play a hugely important role on the Internet; they are used to grab the reader's attention and to encourage people to click on the article. It is also necessary for them to include key words or tag words so that the article can be found on search engines like Google.

The rules for generating a headline are as follows:

- Sum up the article topic
- The headline should never be short or boring
- It should be easy to understand
- It may use relevant catch words
- It must not use lengthy phrases

The rules for generating online teasers are as follows:

- It should entice readers to the story
- It should present the angle of the story clearly
- It should make the reader curious

In terms of the online story, there are generally four ways of analysing them. These are:

1. Information: Is the story easy to understand?

2. Optics: Is the text easily readable? Are there clear subheads and paragraphs?

3. Quality: Remember that the most important information in the story needs to be at the top, and make sure that the story is precise and to the point.

4. Feeling: Is the story enjoyable? Is it entertaining or informative, or both?

CHECKLIST

i.   Does the beginning include the most important information? Have key words plus the five W's and one H been used or answered?

ii.   Is the text short and simple to read? Is all the language used active?

iii. Is a story developed through the text?

iv.   Does the story appeal to its target audience?

v.   Has everything been done to optimize the story for search engines?

vi.   Is all the information purveyed in the article absolutely up-to-date?

vii. Have all the Internet's resources been used, e.g. links to other information and social media?

Mobile Photography –Taking Quality Images

The rise of mobile journalism

Due to the changing times, mobile reporting has become a central part to online journalism. Most smart phones are now fitted with cameras and microphones which allow for recordings which are of a suitable standard to be broadcast.

More ordinary people are able to broadcast and so benefit from high-resolution pictures and sounds as well as journalists.

This initiative was spearheaded by Al Jazeera in 2008, who gave both their staff and 'citizen journalists' smart phones in several Arab states. This was particularly utilized in crisis zones and areas which were hard for journalists to reach.

People were able to post pictures, videos and sound recordings online. So the barriers between being a media producer (trained journalist) and media consumer (citizen journalist) have been eradicated.

Photography on a mobile

The quality of the pictures people are able to take on their phones is always increasing, and accompanied with the use of the right software applications, pictures can be edited on smart phones and then distributed across the Internet.

Mobile journalism is most effectively used when stories need to be either filed quickly or published immediately. It is also good for situations where somebody with a camera might be unwanted.

There are certain steps that any journalist should follow when producing visual material on their smartphone. They are as follows:

1. Recording: The user must ensure that the phone is in a stable position and must take things like perspective and composition

into consideration. The user should attempt to take as many pictures as possible.

2. Editing: mobile applications like Photoshop Express (which is also free) can be used to enhance pictures via cropping, contrast and light levels.

3. Sending or broadcasting: pictures can be sent by MMS (Multimedia Messaging Service), email or through apps like Whatsapp. They can also be posted online quickly thanks to sites like Instagram and Tumblr.

If possible, journalists should avoid using zooming in options on their phone camera because it decreases the picture quality. It's always better to move towards the object you are trying to capture if you need a closer shot.

A phone's flash feature can distort pictures and make them appear badly lit, so avoid using this as well.

CHECKLIST

i.   Make sure battery levels on the phone are good and that the phone's memory has enough data.

ii.   Make sure that the camera is set to photograph at its highest definition / best quality.

iii.   Make sure composition and perspective have been thought about before taking the picture.

iv.   If being publisher later, consider: Do I know the name and spelling of the person I'm photographing? Do I have their permission to take / use the image?

v.   Is there a story within the picture? Does it create curiosity?

Video Production with Smart Phones

Some of the first ever material recorded by a smartphone was used in a TV documentary filmed in Syria in 2012. The footage was sent to Al Jazeera by a reporter.

Later that year, the BBC broadcast an interview from a flooded British bowling club live, using just an iPhone and the software app Dejero Live+.

Applications like iMovie, ReelDirector and Splice are some of the most popular software for making videos that are suitable to be broadcast. Videos can also be edited or live streamed on these apps.

It is also more beneficial if an external microphone and lens can be used to increase the quality of the video.

As was the case with taking photos, there are three things that should be taken into consideration when trying to get the best quality recording. They are:

1. Recording: An interview is an example of a recording. Software like Filmic Pro for the iPhone can be used to measure volume levels.

2. Editing: as previously discussed with photos, it is possible to edit and crop footage on the phone by using apps like iMovie and ReelDirector.

3. Sending or broadcasting: it is possible to send the footage to another device via Wi-Fi and to broadcast it directly online through sites like Youtube and Vimeo.

When considering how to structure/ format a video broadcast, there are a number of different techniques to make the video succinct and precise.

First, journalists should consider a short introduction. This can be achieved by selecting the "front camera" function on the phone and look directly into the lens. Viewers need to be informed of what is happening on site. Make sure that you plan what you want to say at the beginning and end of the video before speaking.

Secondly, a short camera pan is always a good idea. This is done by slowly moving the camera from left to right (or vice versa) in a complete sweep to film the surrounding scene. Always start and finish with a strong focal point.

Finally, to create a short passage of movement that could be used for the introduction to the video, start with a strong focal point and walk a few meters, holding the camera steady, until you reach a final focal point.

There is also now the option of live streaming to broadcast footage from phones on to the Internet. Services like Bambuser, Ustream and the aforementioned Dejero are popular for this. These services will come in the form of apps which need to be installed onto your mobile; you will usually have to register with the service as well. Normally, this is free. The quality of the live stream will be better if the user is connected to wireless Internet on-site.

CHECKLIST

i.   Check battery levels and phone storage. Battery levels are particularly important when making videos because phones require a lot.

ii.   Ensure that when making a video, the phone is in flight mode – otherwise a call could interrupt the filming.

iii.   Make sure that you have a good filmic angle, and when editing the video make sure you have used a meaningful excerpt from the video.

iv.   Attempt to stop the picture from shaking. Tripods can be useful for this.

v.   Remember that the digital zoom tool on a phone camera can decrease the quality.

vi.   Wind can ruin the sound quality on a recording, so make sure the weather conditions you're filming in are suitable.

vii.   A few seconds of silence before and after the recording are advised.

Radio Production with Smart Phones

In 2012, BBC journalist Natalia Antelava won the Foreign Press Association award for a radio broadcast, which she created using only her iPhone.

During the riots in Manchester in 2011, another BBC journalist, Nick Garnett, was able to broadcast the event using a piece of software called Luci Live. Other broadcasters were chased away, while Garnett was able to escape notice by talking into his phone.

Smart phones have become a critical weapon in this kind of reporting. They generally have built in microphones and headphone jacks so that other equipment can be attached to improve the quality of the recording.

Some software applications even offer editing, or enhancing options able to be implemented on the phone itself. The material can then be published immediately.

Software applications like iSaidWhat and Hindenburg are good for recording short audio clips and then sending them. Hokusai is a piece of software that effectively enables the user to edit and work with several recordings at once.

There are three steps for making sure that material recorded on a smart phone is suitable to be broadcast. They are:

1. Recording: use an external microphone and the appropriate software in a situation where the environment could affect your recording.

2. Editing: depending on the software available to you on your phone, you can cut or edit your material on your device.

3. Sending or broadcasting: material and recordings can be sent via Bluetooth, cable or wireless Internet connection to other devices like computers, or can be uploaded online straight away to services such as Soundcloud.

There are various kinds of recordings one can make while on the move, including short introductions, short interviews and recordings of eyewitness accounts.

Today, one can create a complete audio report using the software on a phone; this can include things like mixing audio clips or interviews, editing material and sending it for broadcast through the Internet.

CHECKLIST

i.   Make sure that the phone's microphone is pointed in the direction of the source that is being recorded.

ii.   Make sure that the phone's microphone is not facing the wind.

iii. Remember to check the audio levels before recording.

iv.   Test all the software on the device briefly before recording to ensure it all works.

v.   Make sure that the microphone is close to the person who is speaking.

vi.   Try and mute distracting background noises as much as possible.

vii. Use the headphones to check the quality of the recording.

viii. Record a few seconds of silence at the beginning and end of the material.

The Use of Social Media

Twitter and Facebook have become fundamental in the way that journalism has changed and works today.

The lines between the people who produce the media and their traditional audience have been blurred. There is now more communication between the two parties and social media has been a useful tool in the generation of this new dialogue.

Journalists are enabled by social media to communicate to both their sources and the public quickly, while enabling different ways of research.

Twitter is a good example of a site that is able to broadcast an unfolding story, as users affected may post about it. Often sources on Twitter are quicker than reporters.

Social media is good for acquiring a number of sources that a journalist can deem as trustworthy, and allows them to keep up with chosen sources mostly without having to pay.

Information and opinions from individuals can be gathered more quickly and directly with the use of social media. Individuals can include friends, complete strangers or followers. This is referred to as crowdsourcing.

Social Media is also useful for journalists who want their work to reach the widest possible audience, and can help them find new story ideas.

When using social media the classic five W's and one H questions also apply when dealing with news stories. In this context, these are:

- *What* will add to the value of the story?
- *Who* has written, filmed, recorded or commented on the story?
- *Where* is the part of the story that will grab reader's attention?

- *When* will the audience read the story, and how will they read it? E.g. on a computer? Or on a phone?
- *Why* should Internet users want to read or interact with my work? Why would they want to comment on it?
- *How* do I gain meaningful data and information? And how do I find / use trustworthy sources?

There are some basic codes by which journalists (and users in general) are expected to adhere to in terms of behaviour on social media. Generally these are things like "Think first, then post" and "Don't tell any secrets."

CHECKLIST

i.   Be credible

ii.   Add value

iii. Make sure you stay up-to-date and current

iv.   Stay relevant by publishing regularly

v.   Be authentic

vi.   Answer the people who comment on / interact with your work

vii. Enter into dialogue

Social Media on the Internet

One of the most important things to remember when using social media as a resource for research is that most of the opinions come from people who are private citizens. Unlike journalists, these people are not required to conform to any journalistic checks or provide high quality information.

There are two main guidelines which should be kept in mind when doing research on social media; "From Outside In" and "Deep, Not Wide."

"From Outside In" means that you must initially check the information that you obtain through unbiased and reliable sources outside of social networks. It is only appropriate to use social media for research purposes if these checks have taken place.

"Deep, Not Wide" references the way in which it is possible to get side-tracked when researching on social media. The sheer amount of information available can make it hard to stay focused.

There are some questions that a journalist should always ask themselves before trusting the information they find on social media. These are:

1. Is this information too good to be true?

2. Could the sources be fake?

3. How regularly does the source publish?

4. Has the video or image clearly been tampered with or edited?

It is important to consider context when deciding which sources to trust on social media. A journalist should always ask themselves the following questions when considering this.

1. How long has this particular account existed / been active?

2.　What connections (for example, Facebook friends) does this account have?

3.　Who were the first connections this account gained? Who were the first followers?

4.　Is the source who has talked about this account trustworthy?

5.　Is it possible to contact the owner of this account personally?

6.　Are there any other sources online that could provide information about this account?

When considering how trustworthy a source is on social media, one should always ask themselves the following questions:

1.　What is the appearance of the website address? If the address ends with something like .com or .org then it is far more likely to be trustworthy than something unknown.

2.　Is it possible to use the Who Is tool (whois.domaintools.com) to find out who registered this website?

3.　Can older versions of this website be found by using the Wayback Machine (archive.org/web/)?

CHECKLIST

i.   What is the exact topic of research?

ii.   Who are sources communicating with? Why is this so?

iii.   Is this a trustworthy source?

iv.   What other sources are available to investigate?

v.   Can you contact this source directly?

vi.   How can you verify this source?

vii.   Can you rule out having to use technological manipulations like editing and Photoshopping?

A Web of Change

Edited from 'Why Newspapers Must Change'
by Cordt Schnibben

The internet has created a very different reality for classical media – no longer can print media simply throw their products out to their readers as though they were care packages. The internet makes the readers equal – they become sub-editors, fact-checkers, columnists and an inspiration for media producers, as well as teases, trolls and antagonists at times.

Tablets and smartphones allow users to remain online almost all of the time. This has an impact on the readers, the internet, journalism and even society in general. The user doesn't just read stories; they are continuously feeding the internet with their own texts and pictures.

An online community is evolving whose members no longer require newspapers to debate current affairs or shape their societies. It is a journalism without journalists, enabling people to drive forward their own social movements. Social media like Facebook and Twitter are becoming the conveyors of news, surging ahead of other media.

Yet Twitter and Facebook have virtually no real competitors – the same goes for Google and Amazon. Their home bases are in the hands of US business – a digital-industrial complex that has given rise to new dilemmas around individual privacy. As users of these online giants seek information, orientation and conversation, they are leaving behind a trail of data that has huge commercial (and governmental) value. The result is a kind of capitalist state monopoly; a new form of digital imperialism, which doesn't involve conquering nations but rather networks and minds.

Smartphones and tablets that allow one to always be online function very differently from 20th century mass media. The digital citizen communicates in his or her niche, in networked groups with followers and 'friends'. The digital citizen is a diva, spoilt by possibility and bored with the analogue texts in newspapers that cost too much and stuffed with words that do not interest. The digital citizen wants a customized product – nothing mass produced – and it must be cheap. Free would be best. The digital citizen enjoys things like Snapchat, Huffington Post, BuzzFeed, tumblr and TED.

Newspapers with websites don't feel innovative enough to this digital citizen – often the content is not much different from the print version and the innovative possibilities offered by online media are underutilized. If the media producer were to listen, they would realize that the future newspaper must have the following qualities:-

1. The newspaper has different content – it must be exciting, personalized and service orientated.

2. The newspaper must depart from the idea that it is simply a digital version of what it has in print.

3. Following the previous point, the newspaper must discard the editorial construct of sections, where there are always certain sections in print, even if there is nothing to report.

4. The newspaper must be able to translate its content, form and functions onto a smartphone.

5. The newspaper must engage with readers in a totally different way than print – the readers are now co-producers and sources.

6. Readers should have the option of personalizing the newspaper for themselves, choosing topics that most interest them and subjects they want to be informed about.

7. The newspaper should combine products by journalists with products by bloggers and their readers.

8. Lastly, the newspaper of the future must become more than a medium of news, articles and opinions. It should also help users navigate their everyday realities and it must become what it once was: a public square where opinions and information are freely shared.

Carl Schnibben is an award winning German journalist who has worked for current affairs magazine Der Spiegel since 1998. He has extensively researched how newspapers must reposition themselves in the digital world.

Tips for Boosting Engagement Online

- Ensure that every article has links to social media, with readers being able to retweet and like it on their accounts.

- Readers should be able to comment upon articles easily, but there should be transparent moderation of comments to prevent abuse.

- Use polls that allow readers to 'vote' on certain topics. This can help you to gauge reader's opinions and can inform later articles.

- Use multimedia like videos and audio recordings. Keep an up-to-date YouTube channel.

- Allow readers to shape the context of future articles. Invite contributions for photos, videos and even editorial content. Ask readers what they want to be covered.

- Incentivise contributions with prizes and recognition.

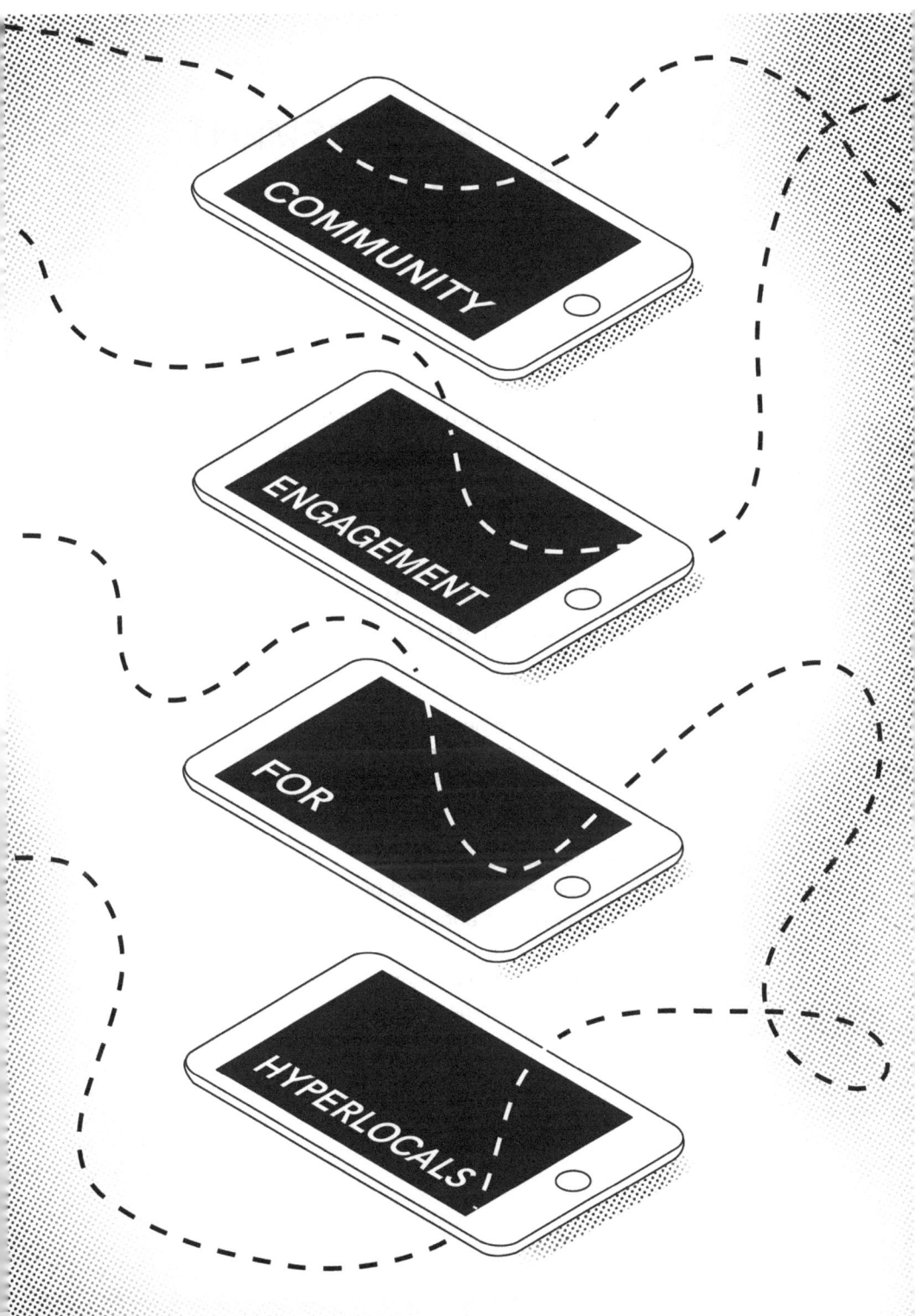

COMMUNITY ENGAGEMENT FOR HYPERLOCALS

* * *

The material below has been edited from the 'Community Engagement and Hyperlocal News' publication by Jonathan Cable et al (cited in the Resources section). Whilst most is a summary, we have also made some additions.

Questions for deciding who your target audience are

Like with any media outlet, you need to know who your readers are – both to ensure that they keep coming back to your site and also to present a case to advertisers. You may wish to consider the following questions: -

1. What do people care about?
2. Where to find stories that interest people?
3. What are people talking about, and where?
4. How to contribute?
5. What kind of content is of interest?
6. Who are the most active people
7. What can be offered that is different to other news or information
8. What kind of engagement is sought?

Social media

Social media is a vital tool for any media outlet and there exists unique opportunities to build engagement for hyperlocal publications.

Twitter

You can search tweets by area and discover which profiles are most active. You can then add these users to a Twitter list. Online sources like 'Topsy' (**www.topsy.com**) allow you to discover trending tweets and profiles. Another tool is 'FollowerWonk' that allows you to search Twitter profiles and bios and discover which are the most active and engaged. Tools like this allow news outlets to uncover a range of interesting and current stories.

When using Twitter, posts should be varied – with a mixture of images, polls, links and videos. Tweets should be 'action based', to the point, and usually involve some kind of image, multimedia or method of engagement.

Facebook

You can search in a similar way on Facebook. However, Facebook in itself is useful for generating greater user engagement within specific geographic areas. It can be a place to start debates on council policies, to seek volunteers for events, or to hold lively polls on the best recipe. Facebook is generally seen as more personal and flexible than Twitter, although both platforms have their advantages and disadvantages.
When using Facebook, it is advisable to be proactive: like other pages, especially those associated with your area or interests; make Facebook posts 'human'; ask questions, and finally continually interact.

Social media stats

- 189 million people access Facebook via their mobile.

- Tweets with an image get twice as much engagement.
- Tweets with hashtags get twice as much engagement.
- Tweets have 12 times better chance of being retweeted if it is asked for, and 23 times higher is the word 'retweet' is written in full.
- In fact, when you make any kind of 'call to action' (whether it be asking for retweets, follows, replies or likes) you are more likely to generate higher engagement.
- Tweets with links are 86% more likely to be retweeted.
- Facebook posts with images receive 56% more likes, 104% more comments and 84% more click-throughs.
- Posting 1-2 times a day gets 40% more engagement, whilst posting 1-4 times a week gets 71% more engagement.

Community Engagement

There are many forms of engagement:

- As promotion or outreach – users consume content.
- To encourage reactions – comments, shares, likes.
- To build participation – people contribute their time.
- To boost civic participation – members address community issues.

It is important to combine offline and online engagement. A media outlet should be at the centre of a community – sponsoring activities, attending events, involved in different initiatives. Show people you are a cog in their community, part of things, with a stake in what is happening – as opposed to being some distant reporter.

Collaborating with others is also important to grow networks and share resources. This can help generate more innovative content and widen engagement.

Online Media Engagement

A media outlet should show interest in people's comments by responding and quoting on social media channels. When engaging with comments, you should sound human and essentially be yourself – rather than an appendage of a faceless media organization.

Having 'calls to action' are also important: state clearly what you want from people. Is it an opinion, or some photos? Continuously asking questions from visitors and readers helps generate content and boosts engagement.

Content should be 'short and snappy', as well as friendly and informal. Posting content should be done regularly to avoid your media outlet looking stagnant and unused.

Social Media Surgeries

A good way of engaging with local people and helping them at the same time is to provide surgeries for people to navigate their way around online and organise their time on social media.

Featured Guest Articles

Attracting and creating content around influential and interest community members is a good tactic. Such local voices can be featured via self-written profiles, interviews, 'Q and A' columns (often in response to other readers) or in-depth articles.

Publicising Upcoming Events

Most people will be interested in what is happening in their area. If they can use your media outlet as the most relevant, comprehensive and up to date source of information for upcoming events then you have a guaranteed audience.

At the same time, organization events can build relationships with organisations and businesses, who may later wish to advertise. Going on to attend events also shows your media outlet as active in the community, whilst providing potential stories.

Breaking News

When a big news story breaks in your area then you should be the first media to report upon it. If others get there before you, or worse still if you completely ignore it, then your reputation as a reliable and useful source of information will be undermined. Keeping an eye on social media (see above) and having a base of active local contacts is key to ensuring that you stay on top of news stories.

Unusual Stories

Sometimes it is the smaller stories with a weird twist that get more attention than 'breaking news'. It could be about an exotic spider trapped in someone's bath tub, or even a tree that looks like a person. Adding photos and videos to such stories boosts their interest immensely. It is not unknown for the unusual stories of hyperlocal media outlets to be sold on to national newspapers.

Cover Local Causes and Campaigns

Local news providers can and should play an active role in covering causes and campaigns in their area. Doing so not only improves relations with campaigners but allows local people to find out and participate in something that may be of immense importance to them. This kind of content mobilises and connects people, who may later come back to your news outlet to keep updated.

However, it is important to adopt a neutral political stance because there are always differing points of view and causes to take into account. This is not to say that a journalist or media outlet cannot take a stance on a particular campaign, but rather to ensure that all the facts (of whatever side) are presented fairly.

A Platform for the Community, Individuals and Groups

A hyperlocal publication can be a way for other people to reach out, providing a platform for artwork, initiatives, campaigns, concerns and more. It is worth developing a strategy that enables people to move from low-level engagement (commenting on posts, retweeting, etc.) to medium-level (contributing content and participating in events) to high-level (working as an editor, coordinating social media, being part of the team).

Such levels of engagement make a media outlet more transparent and welcoming, since it effectively acts like a community organization embedded within the local area. Indeed, many hyperlocal publications are run by groups of local residents, for local residents, with copious opportunities for new people to get involved.

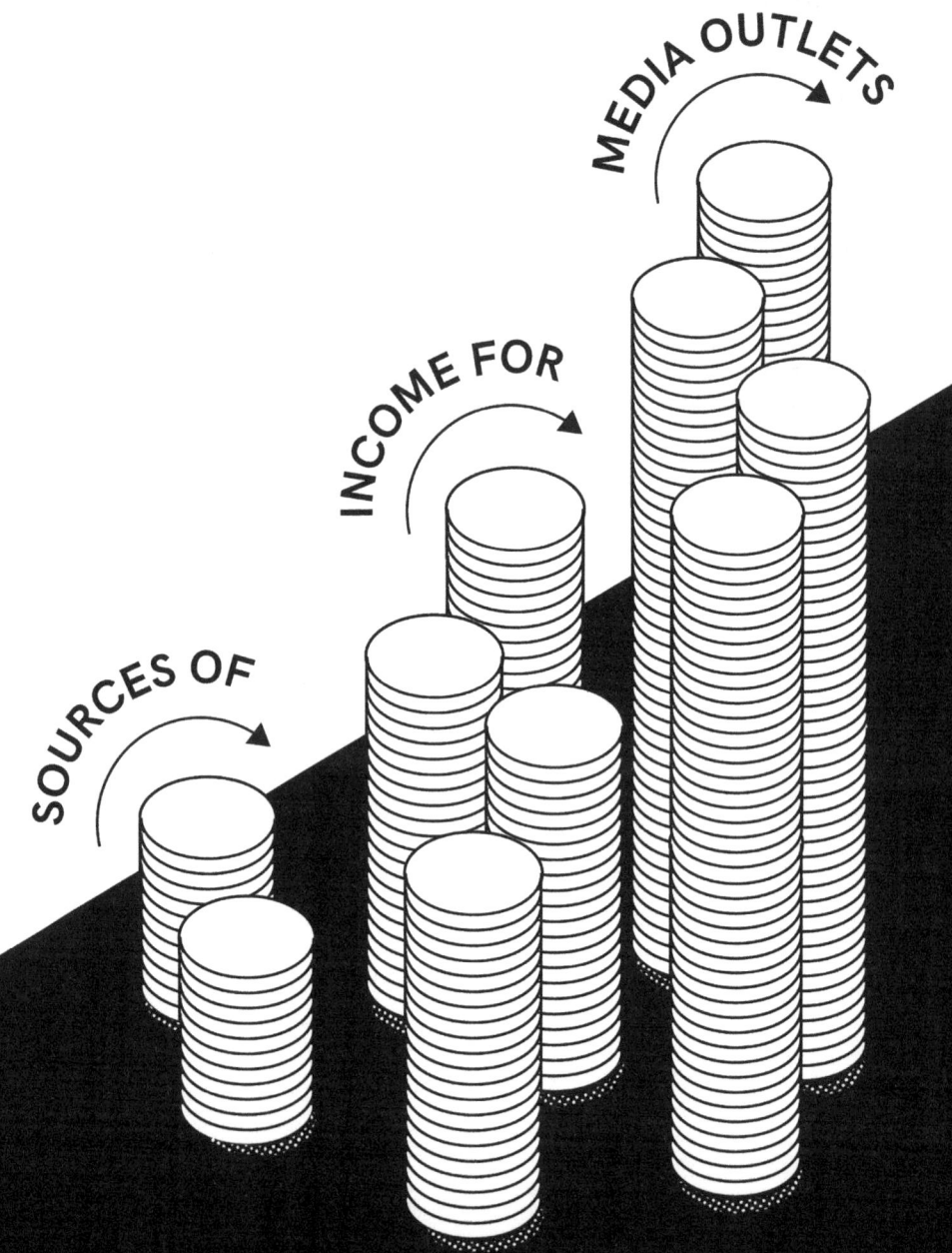

SOURCES OF REVENUE FOR MEDIA OUTLETS

* * *

Advertising

Advertising is fickle and risky: being too dependent on it can undermine the quality and independence of a publication. At the same time, it is one of the hardest sources of income for new publications and media outlets to secure. And yet advertising continues to be one of the central potential income sources for media entrepreneurs, so we have devoted a lot of time to looking at what is involved in securing it.

Why advertise?

Advertising will always remain an income source, since businesses always need to market their products and services. In the UK, around £14 billion is spent on advertising each year and in 2016 over half of this went towards internet advertising. However, there may be different motives for why a business advertises and it is useful to understand these.

Launching new products or services is often the most common reason for advertising. Another reason is if a company wants to differentiate its product or service from competitors.

Other companies use advertising to boost their image as a whole, by making people think more positively about it. Then there might be reasons for companies to advertise in order to get more staff, or even to motivate existing employers.

A key to getting advertising is to understand the needs of the advertise, and present a case why your publication meets these needs.

Advertising in different media

It certainly matters to advertisers whether you are a website, print publication, radio station or television channel. The latter are seen as more widely accessible, since they can reach everyone regardless of social class, age, education or location. Other media, especially print, is more restrictive in that it may often cost money to access, is geographically limited, and is dependent on people being able to read. Websites, whilst easier to access, also risk being 'hidden' and unused since there are so many others available for people to use. This is why advertisers are highly selective in what media they choose: you will never see an advert for Coca Cola in a local newspaper, but you are pretty much guaranteed to see one on television at some point.

Editorial influence

Advertisers will often expect to have some kind of influence over editorial content, whether that be in the aligning of interests (promoting consumerism) or tacit endorsement of products. However, media outlets should be very careful about this.

Any paid advertising should be clearly labelled and demarcated from editorial content: failing to do so not only misleads readers but drives down quality. In the long term, media will only be trusted and accepted by its audience if it proves independence and credibility.

Poorly labelled 'sponsored articles' and artificial reviews serve only to erode the appeal of a publication, ultimately reducing its value to other advertisers.

If a pushy advertiser manages to influence editorial content, or threatens to withdraw some planned adverting, then the best thing to do is just let that advertiser go. Whilst complying with their demands may result in some temporary income, the long-term impact will be the erosion of the readers' trust.

Free advertising

Some media choose to offer free advertising to selected businesses in the hope that they will one day take out a paid advertisement. The problem with this tactic is people tend not to value things that are given for free, especially advertising!

Exceptions to this rule can be when giving free advertising space in a brand new publication, which would otherwise have no advertising, or offering space for charitable organisations.

Sponsorship

A business may sponsor an article or section, and this is generally acceptable as long as it has no influence over the actual content. For example, it may be that a travel company sponsors a weather report, or a bank sponsors a 'Pet Health' supplement.

However, there are also 'advertorials' where the media outlet or journalist is contracted to write a story about a product or service. Advertorials often take the form of positive critiques and are common in printed media. We will take a closer look at advertorials later on.

Marketing departments and media agencies

In larger businesses, there are marketing departments that handle advertising decisions, whereas for smaller ones it is usually the business owner or managing director.

The larger businesses often work with media and advertising agencies. The advertising agency is typically a creative business that develops advertisements, whilst the media agency is responsible for the placement of those advertisements.

The two core roles of the media agency are to develop a media plan and contacting selected outlets to place adverts. The first role involves the agency looking at how best a business can advertise its product: the mix of media (print, TV, etc.); how many advertisements there will be and how long to run them for; formats and sizes of adverts, and so on. The media agency then contacts outlets according to the plan and negotiates with them on price.

Media agency or advertiser?

Building a relationship with both media advertiser and advertiser is equally important, but it should be remembered that advertisers can often change media agencies and also have ultimate control over the brand, product and money. Therefore, cultivating a good relationship with an advertiser is of upmost importance. It is also worth remembering that advertisers can instruct media agencies to get more involved with a particular media outlet.

Understanding media agencies

The operations of media agencies vary widely. Some are absolutely at the service of their clients and do everything possible to help an advertiser achieve the goals set out in their media plan. Others are more focused on their own profit and will tailor advice around obtaining their own financial goals. For this reason they may steer clients towards advertising in more expensive media, in order to justify a higher budget and therefore a higher cut. It is even known for media agencies to negotiate better deals with media outlets, in return for the agency steering more of their clients in that direction. In other words, they guarantee the media outlet their business and are rewarded for that – but the savings they make are not passed back to the advertiser.

Inside a media agency, the most important staff member for media outlets to know is the 'media planner'. These individuals negotiate directly with the media outlets and their advertising clients. Their recommendations make the difference between a business placing an advert in your media outlet, or someone else's.

There are also 'media buyers', who negotiate prices for advertising spaces. It is always advisable to work directly with media planners, where possible, since it is the planners that are able to garner information that will be passed onto their clients. All the buyers are concerned about is pricing.

Overall, those working for media agencies will be young, communications-savvy, and trained to analyse market data. Their critical considerations are circulation, readership and reach. At the same time, some media agencies are interested in visions, stories and endeavours – in media outlets that stand apart.

Competition between media agencies

The world market for advertising is currently dominated by just five major agencies, which have many different subsidiaries. A media owner can come into contact with around 20 different agencies, but there is a high likelihood that all of these work under the auspices of 'the big five'. However, there are also smaller independent agencies working within every country and their market share of local advertising differs immensely.

Considerations for Advertisers

Try to put yourself in the shoes of an advertiser. What kind of things might they consider before advertising in a publication? Here are some:

- Why is the media product essential for my audience?

- What is it about the media product that makes it so relevant to my audience's lives?

- What makes the media product unique and sets it apart?

- What makes my target audience unique?

Looking at these questions is important, and you need to be in the position to answer them.

Then there are other factors, which an advertiser may themselves not think about. For example, whether a publication is actually read, valued and trusted. It is all very well for a free newspaper to have a huge circulation, but if it is just picked up briefly and then thrown away then it has little value. Compare that with a newspaper that has a cover price and smaller circulation, which is read with interest and passed on to other readers, and this is clearly the better option for the advertiser even though the circulation is lower.

Notwithstanding such scenarios, circulation remains the most important factor in advertisers' minds. For digital products, the equivalent is 'unique visitors' (how many new people visit a web page, and also how long they actually stay on that page).

Circulation Data

It is also important for an advertiser to know how often something is published and how it is distributed. Is it a newspaper sold via kiosks or street sellers? Are subscription services available and, if so, what differentiates subscribers from on-street buyers?

It is important to assure potential advertisers and media agencies that circulation and readership figures are accurate. This can be done by getting a printer to independently verify how many copies are printed, or another third party such as a lawyer. Another way is to get an audit of a publication's accounting records, to show many copies of a publication were sold.

Beyond Circulation

If other publications have higher circulations then it does not mean an advertiser will automatically favour them. Your publication may attract more of the advertiser's audience; it may have a more suitable geographic reach; or the ethos and content may more closely align with the advertisers than that or a lager media outlet.

The 'Cost Per Thousand'

The cost per thousand or CPM is calculated by taking the price of advertising and dividing it by the circulation. Publications with a higher circulation and/or lower advertising cost will have a lower CPM. However, advertisers do not base their decisions solely on CPM: it is possible to have a smaller circulation and higher advertising cost because a publication reaches a certain type of audience, or is more likely to be read.

Target market

It is essential to know your audience or target market in order to successfully engage with advertisers and media agencies. You need to be able to define them in terms of age, political preference, gender, location, income and other factors. The more you know about them, the better.

It is the content of your publication that defines your target market. Surveys, questionnaires and opportunities for readers to provide comment and feedback are good ways to get data on your target market. When approaching prospective advertisers, it is very useful to put this data into an advertising pack.

Bear in mind that advertisers are always looking for new and innovative ways to engage their customers, so highlight any ways that your publication might do this – narrowing it down to a specific group of people.

Closing an Advertising Deal

For media start-ups, approaching new advertisers can be daunting. You need to be able to forge a relationship, whilst holding your ground in the event an advertiser tries to influence editorial content.

The best way to start getting advertisers is to look at your target market (see previous section) and the kinds of businesses that relate to them. For example, a women's fashion magazine would be wasting its time trying to contact men's outdoor sport companies.

Once you have an idea of which advertisers may be interested in your product, the next step is to do some initial research on each. What makes the advertiser unique? Why might they prefer your product over others? Are they launching anything new?

After this, you need to call the company's main office and find out who is responsible for advertising and marketing. Alternatively, you may be able to get a contact and number via the company's website. Your goal is to arrange a time to meet with them, when you can fully introduce your media product.

Trying to progress an advertising lead by email is usually a waste of time, especially if your email is unsolicited and they do not know you.

Introducing Yourself

When calling someone, make sure you introduce yourself. Give them your name, position and the company you work for. The ideal scenario is for the most senior person in your media organisation to speak with the most senior person in the advertiser's organisation. That way, decisions can be made without anyone else having to relay information.

You need to explain, precisely and briefly, what your media organisation does and why you are calling.
It could be something like:

We are a national magazine that covers environmental issues.

Or

We are a local newspaper for Upton.

Anything that your outlet does better and makes it unique should be presented during this brief conversation. You must be clear that you are not contacting them about an interview or story, but rather about marketing and advertising.

Your end goal of this call – getting a face to face meeting – is best secured when you connect with the interests of the advertiser and make your media outlet stand out.

What to know

You don't need to throw tons of data and numbers at someone over the phone, but you should have the key information about your publication to hand.

If your circulation is particularly high, that should certainly be mentioned. Or if you are the only publication for a specific area, that is also good to remark upon.

Once at the meeting, ensure you bring all relevant information with you. This includes copies of your publication, advertising pack, and ideally a short presentation.

Make sure you leave time and space for a real conversation as well: be friendly and engaging.

Deciding on cost

The easiest way to decide the cost of your advertising is to look at similar publications and their cost per thousand. Your costs should not be too high above this, but at the same time it would be wrong to put them much below.

If there is no real competition, then you can undertake the following steps: -

- How much money do you need to keep your organisation running?

- How many advertising slots would you need to sell in order to raise this money?

- These two figures will allow you to determine the cost of advertising space.

Generally, the more elite and inaccessible an audience is to advertisers, the higher you can charge for advertising.

Negotiation

All advertisers will be looking for a special deal or some kind of discount. It is therefore sometimes a good tactic to produce an advertising pack with prices higher than the actual ones you normally sell for.

You should be open to negotiation and tweak discounts according to the size of advertisers and whether they are willing to advertise for longer periods.

The ideal scenario is to get a base of strong repeat advertisers, rather than going out to continually find new ones.

Expectations

Once you get an advert, you should ensure that it meets the advertiser's expectations. The size, look and placement of an advert should not deviate from what the advertiser specified and supplied. It is wise to send them a PDF or screen shot of what their advert will look like before it goes live or sent for printing.

Once produced, the advertiser will expect copies of the publication with their advert inside. When sending these, a media owner can accompany it with a signed letter thanking the advertiser for their choice and a small gift. Advertisers can also be invited to launch events.

If they have not booked adverts in later editions, you should contact a previous advertiser to ask if they would like to place another advert.

Payment

Many advertisers pay promptly, but sadly many others do not. In fact, it is usual for most media outlets to at some point be forced to chase advertisers to pay.

Advertisers should be afforded a full month's payment period, and this should be clearly stated in an invoice when they book an advert.

Once this time elapses, a polite reminder email should be sent – followed by a call, if necessary. If, after two weeks, you still do not hear from the advertiser then a more formal email should be sent. In the UK, invoices that are unpaid after one month can have a late payment fee added – something that should be made clear to advertisers who don't pay after 50 days.

It is not unknown for media outlets to send a pre-action protocol letter to advertisers who do not pay (the first step before commencing court proceedings) but it is rare for advertisers to let it go beyond this, unless their business is genuinely bankrupt.

Advertorials

As noted earlier, sometimes it is not enough for a business to simply buy space in a publication but to have some kind of editorial reference. An advertorial is usually written by a media outlet or journalist, after receiving payment from the business to write something positive.

Whilst advertorials can generate more income than just adverts, since they are valued more, it is important that they be properly demarcated from pure editorial content. If this doesn't happen then readers will lose trust and interest.

Another way of presenting advertorials is to make them into inserts within a publication, which are clearly separate from the rest of the content.

CHECKLIST

i.   Is the advertorial clearly marked and demarcated from other editorial content?

ii.   Has the advertiser not influenced other content in the publication?

iii. Does the advertorial align with the general ethos of the publication, and contents thereof?

Listings and Directories

Media outlets can create listings and directories for all manner of things: jobs, local businesses, obituaries, events, and so forth.

A form of advertising, these can also be informative to readers, whether someone is looking for something to do on the weekend or a nearby plumber.
A media outlet can introduce listings and directories freely, then phase in 'enhanced' or 'highlighted' entries for businesses willing to pay.

Another way of using listings and directories is to encourage businesses to offer special discounts to readers.

Case Study: The Lincolnite

The Lincolnite, a hyperlocal publication in the North of England, lists jobs and properties via a plug-in and charges between £80-£200 for a jobs listing (for 14-30 days), with properties listed on a monthly subscription.

They work with three agents currently (and are looking to expand) and they get to choose how many properties/pages are required. They also have paid options for event advertising, but do list events for free too.

Membership Models

Membership schemes allow readers to support or even to co-own media outlets.

This can work by people subscribing to become members, contributing a small monthly or yearly amount to a media outlet, and in return receiving certain benefits or incentives.

The other form of membership is where people own shares of a media outlet, which is a cooperative.

Case Study: The Bristol Cable

The Bristol Cable is a media cooperative in Bristol, UK made up of over 2000 members. Each member contributes a minimum of £1 per month, with the average paying around £3. Once they become a member, they can join in with online discussions that decide on the newspaper's content and general direction. There are also regular meetings updates by email, and special discounts with participating businesses.

Through this model, the Bristol Cable is being able to cover its print costs from memberships and is also paying coordinators and contributors.

Podcasts

Short (30-60 second-long) podcasts can be sold to a range of businesses and events. A hyperlocal publisher might, for example, use the online magazine 'Slate' Panoply model to work with partners on creating custom or native podcasts, delivering helpful and entertaining information to listeners.

Case Study: Chicago Podcast Cooperative

The Chicago Podcast Cooperative, based in North America, produces 30 shows from a shared studio resource and sells advertising across its collection of shows, bringing together local podcasts and local businesses. Software like audioBoom and SoundCloud offer simple mobile-to-web audio recording options.

Crowdfunding

An increasingly popular funding method, crowdfunding allows large groups of people to contribute money towards supporting a publication or media outlet.

People who contribute usually expect some kind of incentive or gift, which could be a free copy of a publication or more elaborate things like tickets to special events or even free advertising.
There are many different crowdfunding platforms, some of which offer 'match funding' from charitable sources.

Media outlets can use crowdfunding to launch, to support new editions, or even to form a new constitution.

Crowdfunding is also a useful way to spread awareness of a publication and can encourage other forms of support.

Case Study: The New Internationalist

The New Internationalist is a UK magazine covering a range of issues. At the end of 2016, the New Internationalist launched an ambitious crowdfunding campaign that involved giving people shares of the organisation in return for their financial support. The publication raised over £100,000 in finance to sustain itself and develop a growth strategy.

Grant Funding

Although competitive and never guaranteed, it is possible for some media outlets to get support from grant funding – especially if they serve disadvantaged communities that lack any other form of effective communication mechanism.

It is important to note that 'media outlets' do not just have to be about providing news to people, they can also be a component of the community and provide a range of services and activities. This can include providing journalism training to local young people, updating community noticeboards, or providing ways for residents to become directly involved in a publication.

Grant funders are looking for organisations that generate meaningful social impact and which do not operate for profit. It is totally possible to be constituted in this way and still be able to receive a salary.

Case Study: Vocalise

Vocalise is a hyperlocal community magazine covering three parishes in Bristol, UK. As well as producing a magazine, Vocalise also manages the area's community noticeboards and acts as an overall organisational body. Early in its inception, Vocalise received a Big Lottery grant and then went on to secure funding from a range of sources to help deliver projects around community journalism workshops, social cohesion, residents meetings, and more.

Copy Sales

Generally, print publications make around half of their income from the sale of copies – and the other half from advertising. However, this is changing as lots of printed media has no cover price.

Where a publication does have a price, it is essential that this is set at the right amount. To begin with, this can be a difficult task. The only way of truly finding out is to trial the publication and see how many copies are left.

There are many ways of selling but the two main ones are on the streets through vendors, or via retailers. In both cases you need to set a price that allows the vendor or retailer to take a cut without you making a loss. Alternatively, you need to make enough from sales and advertising in order to pay vendors a set hourly salary.

Case Study: The Big Issue

One of the UK's best known street magazines, the Big Issue is sold by homeless vendors who keep 50% of the cover price. The magazine was setup by Derrick Bird in London and went on to spread across the UK, making Bird a lot of money. It is now managed by a charity that is investing into other social enterprises.

Big Issue vendors typically make between £20-£70 per day, with an equivalent amount going to the publisher.

Donations

Media outlets can make a call for donations both before and during their operations.

Donations really only work if you have a large body of supporters, readers or subscribers who are willing to help you raise awareness of a campaign.

Subscriptions

Subscriptions can be the bedrock of a publication, especially for magazines and a lot of online media. However, they take time to grow.

A good method of phasing in subscriptions is to offer access to free content for an initial period, or to let readers access the first part of articles. In order to read more, they need to pay.

Online, there are a variety of 'paywalls' that can be easily deployed. Payment software like Steady also allows you to collect online payments without difficulty and only takes a small commission when someone subscribes.

Once you have subscribers you should ensure that your content is fresh, dynamic and interesting – remember the reasons people are subscribing is because they actually enjoy reading what your media outlet writes about, and what it represents.

Case Study: The Times

The Times is one of the UK's leading national newspapers and has developed an online subscription model to boost digital income. It used a paywall that charges readers between £6-£8 per week, although there are also one-off deals and promotions. Since introducing the paywall and digital subscription model, the Times has gone from operating at a loss to be being the only UK national broadsheet to make a profit (which it has done for the last two years).

Promotional Services

A business is launching a new product and is looking for ways to promote it. Maybe they want to advertise in your publication, but then again maybe you can offer them other support.

As a media outlet, you are in a strong position to help the business with promotion via social media, as well as providing practical assistance and guidance with implementing a promotional strategy.

For example, maybe you could assist with writing press releases and providing contact details for other media outlets. Or maybe you could even produce some leaflets or videos for them.

Promotional services like this can be a good way to supplement other income streams.

Events and Workshops

Launching a new publication or edition is a good reason to put on an event, and these can in themselves generate income. Maybe people need tickets to come to the event, which offers a variety of entertainment. It might, for example, have a buffet ('Dine with the Publisher') or live music.

Nor are events restricted solely to new launches: you could put on events to coincide with a visiting celebrity (make sure they come!) or for more structured activities, such as seminars or debates.

You could look at organising tours in cooperation with local businesses, showing visitors around a particular area. Media audiences like to travel on educational, thematic or city tours that are recommended by their favourite publication.

In a similar way, media outlets are well placed to deliver a range of workshops – from using social media to becoming a community journalist. In many cases other organisations and institutions are in a position to pay for these workshops.

Case Study: Alphens

The magazine Alphens, which is based in the Netherlands, has developed a lucrative income from event ticket sales. Alphens sells tickets for third party events such as Culinary Alphen, Summer at the Lake, Lakeside (dance event), a boxing gala and Restaurant Week. Revenues are approximately €15,000 per year as they get a share of the revenues.

Publishing Services

Individuals, organisations and businesses can contract you to assist them with publishing services. This could include producing digital platforms, magazines and books.

In order to get these services, you must either contact people directly or advertise that your provide this kind of service in your publications and on your website – preferably both.

It can be a potentially lucrative income source if handled well.

Case Study: Arkbound

Arkbound started as a publishing social enterprise in 2015, producing books and magazines. It went on to generate a steady income from book publishing services – providing people with ways in which they could successfully publish books – and this allowed the organisation to continue producing magazines (which would otherwise be making a loss).

Statutory Notices

Some media outlets, particularly larger ones, manage to obtain income from statutory notices. In the UK, the money spent on these notices averages between £45-50 million a year.

Public authorities have a legal obligation to advertise about certain services and planning, but they tend only to do this in larger 'local newspapers' as opposed to smaller hyperlocal publications. That said, it is still possible to present a case to local authorities for them to include statutory notices in your publication.

Many media outlets have managed to secure notices from the NHS (for example, from clinics and screening services) as well as the police and fire service. But at a time of public service cuts, this area of income is increasingly difficult to get.

Sponsorship

Similar to advertising and advertorials, it is possible to get businesses and organisations to sponsor articles and coverage of issues. Where this can go further is when an entire publication, even a media outlet as a whole, is sponsored.

Such wider sponsorship can occur when a media outlet offers to place the logo of an organisation in its inside front page and on the website home page. Frequent mentions of the organisation can also be made via social media, and other forms of promotional assistance such as coverage at events.

Sponsorship is common for media outlets with an ethical or community focus, with the sponsoring organisations supporting that outlet in order to boost their own brand image. It can often be combined with corporate social responsibility aims.

Case Study: Marsactu

French-based Marsactu is a news website and weekly newsletter focused on the city of Marseille. The service was re-launched in 2015 after a successful crowd-funding campaign. Today Marsactu offers sponsoring options of talk shows: a weekly talk show about a specific theme (culture, health, science etc.) where the advertiser can append their logo in return for payment. They have produced about 50 talks a year.

Training and Consultancy

The longer a media outlet exists, the more skills and experience it builds upon and enlarges. Many of these are attractive to organisations, individuals and institutions that want to improve their own knowledge of the media industry or selected areas therein.

A well established media outlet with a good reputation can offer training and consultancy services to a range of clients. These can be combined with workshops and ongoing advice. It may be limited to assisting an organisation to develop a PR strategy, or helping an educational institution to deliver journalism training.

The range of these services is indeed vast, and they can form a lucrative income stream if developed properly.

Selling Content

Syndication is a huge field in itself and involves media outlets buying and selling news stories. Some of the largest media outlets have come to rely on external syndicates that provide them with content, rather than employing journalists who go out and get stories.

An established media outlet, or even a new one, that generates new and 'cutting edge' stories has a good chance of selling its content – either to individual news outlets or to new syndication sites. Every news outlet should be aware of this avenue and have an idea of who to approach in the event that a suitable story is made.

Case Study: Angers Magazine

Angers Magazine, which has a paper and digital publication covering the French city of Angers, has syndicated occasionally – in one case, for an event that created a lot of buzz on their website. The national press and some TV channels wanted to use their photos and videos.

Special Merchandise

Media outlets that are community rooted and with large followers can produce special merchandise for events or selected campaigns. T-shirts, mugs, CDs, bookmarks, posters, stickers, calendars – there is really no limit to what can be produced.

Merchandise can be sold to subscribers, given away as gifts to advertisers or sponsors, or sold through intermediary shops or at events.

Whilst the income potential of merchandise is rarely large, it can provide a nice supplementary source of money and also helps boost the awareness and engagement of a publication.

Collaboration

Arguably the most important of all, collaboration is not solely an income source but should underpin the foundation and ethos of any functioning media outlet.

With the UK media industry being dominated by a handful of large corporations, the best way that smaller ones can succeed is by joining forces with other independent outlets – sharing knowledge, skills, expertise and even operational requirements.

Collaboration can take all shapes and forms – from making joint funding applications and sharing content, to forming collective hyperlocal networks and cross-deploying staff.

It has been consistently demonstrated that media outlets that enter into collaborations have a much better chance of success and sustainability than those that don't.

Case Study: The City Talking

Leeds-based 'The City Talking' has partnered with regional publisher Johnston Press. 'The City Talking' is distributed inside the Yorkshire Evening Post once a month on a Friday. The advertising inventory is sold by Johnston Press, with advertising revenue paid back to 'The City Talking'. The arrangement is mutually beneficial, combining reach, content and resources. In the same city, a group of hyperlocal publishers have harnessed informal links to develop the idea of combining reach, to scale and offer advertising that can be sold across all platforms as a package.

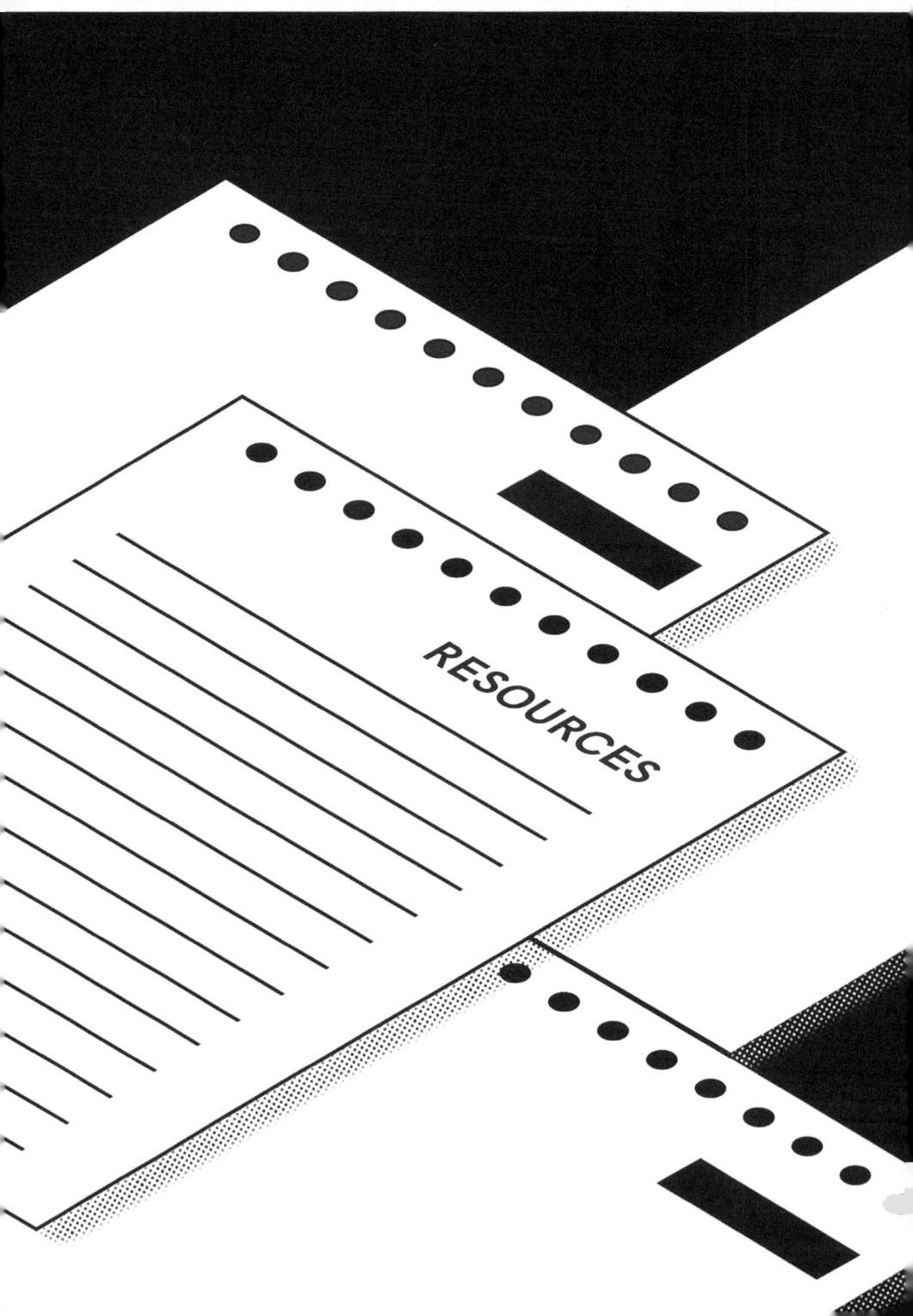

RESOURCES

RESOURCES

* * *

Online resources are rapidly changing, so some of the below may be redundant or unsuitable, with additional ones being created all the time.

Listing of the below sites is not a tacit endorsement.

News Sites (National and International)

Earth Journalism Network (http://earthjournalism.net/stories) – provides up-to-date environmental news from around the world
Climate News Network (http://climatenewsnetwork.net/stories/) – as above, with more global focus on specific categories. Click on an area of interest to get latest news.
Full Fact (https://fullfact.org) – a free fact checking resource for claims made in the media and by public figures.
European Journalism Centre (http://ejc.net/) – a useful resource about European journalism initiatives.
journalism.co.uk (https://www.journalism.co.uk/) - news and opportunities for the journalism industry, focused on the UK
Leak Websites (http://leakdirectory.org/index.php/Leak_Site_Directory#Established_Leak_Sites) – a comprehensive list of websites that provide information on cutting-edge 'leaks' that can be used for (considered) stories.

'Anonymous' (http://anonhq.com/) – US focused, but with occasional cutting edge international stories from the notorious 'anonymous' hacker's network.

Ethical Journalism Network (http://ethicaljournalismnetwork.org/en) - the Ethical Journalism Network provides an assortment of news and resources for journalists who want their work to be used for the benefit of society and the environment. You can subscribe to their newsletter and get updates on specific issues.

Centre for International Media Ethics (http://www.cimethics.org/home/) - similar to above, but focuses on providing training and workshops to journalists. Mention Arkbound when you contact them.

IndyMedia (https://www.indymedia.org/or/index.shtml) – a comprehensive source of information from independent, unbiased journalists reporting around the world. Often 'radical' but insightful stories are featured that are ignored by the mainstream press. Also linked in with other organisations. Their UK site is https://www.indymedia.org.uk/ , which in turn has local subdivisions.

CorporateWatch (https://corporatewatch.org/) – there's always some corporation up to no good, and this website combines innovative methods of journalism (including 'hactivism') with whistleblowing sources to give you the next shocking corporate scandal.

Democracy Now (http://www.democracynow.org/) – another independent global news site untainted by the more corporately-aligned news feeds. Often possible to find gripping stories ignored by the mainstream press.

Reuters (http://uk.reuters.com/) – major news agency used by most newspapers.

Media Wise (http://www.mediawise.org.uk/) – exists to provide free advice and assistance to people who have suffered from bad press coverage, along with ethical journalism training and other support.

Key Resources

https://www.facebook.com/journalists/
These free e-learning courses will help journalists get the most out of Facebook, and each is designed with an emphasis on the three core pillars of the news cycle: discovering content, creating stories and building an audience.

[Facebook tips: When you post, tag people, places and organisations so the post can appear in their timeline, thereby gaining greater coverage.
Posts should be timely, relevant, conversational and authentic. They should be 'live', with a social connection that makes it easier for the audience to engage with.]

https://www.letsgather.in/
Gather is a collection of searchable resources. It's a place to learn (and borrow) from existing projects. It's a hub for collaboration. It's an advanced how-to guide for engagement vets and an on-ramp for newbies. It's a digital meeting space where engaged journalism's budding community of practice can continue to grow and evolve.

https://www.coralproject.net/users/publishers.html
Tools for managing readers' engagement on your website. Currently free: must be downloaded and can then be used as plugins on Wordpress websites.

http://matter.vc
They are looking for start-up media projects that inform, connect, and empower society. Based in New York City and San Francesco, eligible projects must attend one of their accelerators over a course of 20 weeks.

http://solutionsjournalism.org/resources/
Solutions journalism aims to present stories that offer solutions to social and environmental problems. You can join their network and access a range of resources.

https://newslab.withgoogle.com/
Google News Labs offer a powerful range of tools to convey stories, utilise data, build engagement, and discover innovative methods to reach new audiences. The website provides a selection of free, interactive tutorials.

https://learndigital.withgoogle.com/digitalgarage/
A collection of free training resources to improve your knowledge – from social media to SEO.

https://www.carnegieuktrust.org.uk/project/neighbourhood-news/
A series of reports and case studies about how hyperlocal publications can be successful.

Freedom of Information

A powerful statutory tool for seeking the disclosure of information from public bodies, the Freedom of Information Act 2000 was one of the enduring positive legacies of the last Labour government towards open government. https://www.gov.uk/make-a-freedom-of-information-request/the-freedom-of-information-act provides comprehensive information on how to do so.

Photography sites and image formatting

Deviantart (http://www.deviantart.com/) – search for images at the top (where the magnifying glass is), lots of different images available, remember to credit source as appropriate

Stock Free Images (http://www.stockfreeimages.com/) – lots of free images to use, as above
Google Images (set the license rights to 'reuse')

Pexels (https://www.pexels.com/) - a compendium of high quality photos for free use.

Pixabay (https://pixabay.com/)

Wikimedia (https://commons.wikimedia.org/wiki/Main_Page)

Ipiccy (http://ipiccy.com/ - if you don't have image formatting software like Abode Photoshop there is a free alternative with Ipiccy. It is easy to use and provides lots of formatting options.

Search Engine Optimisation

SEO Clerk (https://www.seoclerk.com/) – provides a comprehensive range of cheap services to improve website rankings and social media.

Fiverr (https://www.fiverr.com) – provides similar services, as well as a range of other ones like graphical design.

TOR

Much maligned by the mainstream Press and Governments across the world, TOR ('The Onion Relay) provides a means for people to browse the internet anonymously and communicate with greater privacy (https://www.torproject.org/).

Various news/sources sites like http://gjlng65kwikileax.onion/ (a better version of WikiLeaks) are available but you require a 'TOR' browser for accessing 'onion' sites. If you are going to work with sensitive confidential sources and looking into 'underground' leaks then you should familiarise yourself with TOR, together with message encryption and more secure email facilities.

Consider, for example **CryptoCat** (a secure message program) and **mail2tor** (secure emailing), together with **PGP encryption** (message encryption). Only the most intrepid journalists who work with whisteblowers (for example) will usually require TOR.

Further Reading

The book can only hope to give a brief guide to journalism, so we highly recommend that you read further afield to gain more insights and ideas. The following publications are particularly recommended:-

Cook, C, Geels, K and Bakker, P *'Hyperlocal Revenues in the UK and Europe'* **(2016), NESTA, London.**

Cable, J et al *'Community Engagement and Hyperlocal News: A practical guide'* **(2015), Centre for Community Journalism, Cardiff.**

APPENDIX A: 'The National Union of Journalists' Code of Conduct for Journalists

A journalist will: -

1. At all times upholds and defends the principle of media freedom, the right of freedom of expression and the right of the public to be informed.
2. Strives to ensure that information disseminated is honestly conveyed, accurate and fair.
3. Does her/his utmost to correct harmful inaccuracies.
4. Differentiates between fact and opinion.
5. Obtains material by honest, straightforward and open means, with the exception of investigations that are both overwhelmingly in the public interest and which involve evidence that cannot be obtained by straightforward means.
6. Does nothing to intrude into anybody's private life, grief or distress unless justified by overriding consideration of the public interest.
7. Protects the identity of sources who supply information in confidence and material gathered in the course of her/his work.
8. Resists threats or any other inducements to influence, distort or suppress information and takes no unfair personal advantage of information gained in the course of her/his duties before the information is public knowledge.
9. Produces no material likely to lead to hatred or discrimination on the grounds of a person's age, gender, race, colour, creed, legal status, disability, marital status, or sexual orientation.
10. Does not by way of statement, voice or appearance endorse by advertisement any commercial product or service save for the promotion of her/his own work or of the medium by which she/he is employed.

11. A journalist shall normally seek the consent of an appropriate adult when interviewing or photographing a child for a story about her/his welfare.
12. Avoids plagiarism.

APPENDIX B:
Other Ways to Make Money with Journalism

Shaerpa produced a document entitled 'Financing Quality Journalism' and in noted 52 revenue streams for journalism outlets. Some of these overlap with the ones already noted above, but all are summarized below: -

Advertising: Traditional display or bannering

Book publishing: Use or re-use expertise and brand to publish in book form

Brand spinoff - media: Strong brands are able to broaden their offering under the brand by creating spinoffs such as a yearbook, a special edition, a trade publication for a specific sector or even games

Brand spinoff – other: Certain media brands might take advantage of their strength by moving into other sectors: for example, themed travel with NRC Handelsblad, or a Quote restaurant

Branded content – delivery: Use delivery channels to distribute branded or commercial content. TPO Talk is an example where commercial parties deliver their messages in a narrative form, beyond the familiar advertorial

Branded content – production: Produce or create content for commercial organizations (see previous item)

B2B-B2C differentiation: Re-use content in both B2B and B2C markets. For example, NRC Handelsblad might introduce a special "Finance" platform for the business sector

Classifieds – horizontal: Offer a broad selection of classifieds, comparable to eBay; this requires significant penetration in a wide variety of market segments

Classifieds – vertical: Offer sector-, discipline- or audience-specific classifieds. Media with specialized expertise might introduce classifieds for their sector. For example, OneWorld has the largest job search site for the non-profit sector

Consultative journalism – research: Commercial organizations could perform traditional research or ask journalists to create investigative productions in a consulting capacity

Cooperation – academia: Work with resources, data and people from universities, which might also provide office space and other resources. This creates cost advantages and depth of information

Cooperation – commercial research organizations: Work with resources, data and people from consulting firms or institutes, which might also provide office space and other resources.

Cooperation – crowd journalism: Collaborate with other journalists or the public across national borders, disciplines or areas of expertise (data research-narrative-technology)

Data – archive monetization: Resell high-end archive material, comparable to LexisNexis

Data – semi-finished products: Sell the building blocks for journalistic productions. For example, a piece about demographics in India that another journalist can use in a piece on the upcoming elections in India

Data - lists and rankings: Create and sell lists and rankings

Data – polls and data scraping: Conduct audience polls or scrape data for analysis. With enough reach, journalists can use their audiences to generate survey data on specific topics

Data – sales of: Sell or resell datasets you have created

Data – predefined source lists: Build, manage and sell lists of potential sources and experts. Expert journalists will have lists of and access to the key sources in specific domains; these can be monetized if other media seek those sources

Data – trending analysis: Create and manage trend information. See Data – polls

Donations – corporate: Commercial organizations donate to fund productions or infrastructure

Donations – public: Similar to crowd-funding but not item-specific. Where crowd-funding applies to specific productions, a journalist or platform might seek donations in this model

Events: Create events to generate sponsor and attendee revenues

Government – in-kind support: Governments can provide basic needs, such as office space

Government – subsidies: Governments can directly subsidize productions

Grants – philanthropy: Grants from horizontal or vertical philanthropists

Grants – NGOs: Topic-based grants from NGOs

Product placement: Paid listings of in-article use, non-spot

Product reviews – reselling: Reviews of products and paid links to resellers

Reader revenue – crowd-funding: Possibly equity-based cofunding and co-ownership of outlets or productions

Reader revenue – memberships: Memberships as subscription-plus model

Reader revenue – per article: Readers pay to access a specific production

Reader revenue – retailing: Offer products for sale. For example, OneDayOnly is a retail proposition by NRC Handelsblad

Reader revenue – stand sales: Traditional newsstand sales per issue

Reader revenue – subscription: Traditional subscriptions; possible differentiation of levels

Reselling of developed technological infrastructure: Offer proprietary tools or technology to other parties

Retailing – collective buying: Collectively buy products or services amongst readers

Sell options on film rights: Journalistic cooperative might option film rights to film/documentary makers

Services – auctions: Organize auctions whose revenues will be used to finance journalistic productions

Services – conference speaker (direct or management of): Be hired as a conference speaker or collectively offer journalists who can be hired as speakers

Services – consulting: Reuse expertise and network for high-end, one-on-one consulting

Services – content as a service: Provide content that supports a specific activity, directly to consumers or through outlets

Services – insourcing/pay-rolling: Assume the employer role for journalists made redundant

Services – mediate user forums: Curate user platforms for commercial organizations

Services – network management: Curate, build, manage and monetize a network in your sector of expertise

Services – outsourcing/temping: Offer temp agency service to media-producing organizations

Services – training: Offer training courses or be hired as trainer

Special editions/extra commercial editions: Annual theme, vertical subjects or commercial

Sponsoring – financial: Financial support for productions or editorial domains

Sponsoring – in-kind: In-kind support for production or editorial domain

Syndication – international: Resell productions (original or translated) abroad

Syndication – national: Resell productions nationally Transfer fee for journalist leaving when a journalist leaves for another organization, they or the new employer pay a transfer fee

About the Arkbound Foundation

The Arkbound Foundation exists to widen access to literature and the media for people from diverse and disadvantaged backgrounds. The Foundation seeks to stimulate a vibrant, inclusive democratic society where the press is used as an instrument to enlighten and educate people – serving the needs of the many rather than the few.

We work with people from traditionally excluded backgrounds to help get their work published – in books, magazines and other media - linking them up with experienced mentors and providing a range of workshops in disadvantaged areas.

Since our inception in early 2017 we have been developing a Regional Editors' Network that empowers people to start their own media outlets, and to gain placements in existing media. Based in the UK, we work with partners across the world to build better futures for people who might otherwise be excluded, and to bridge divides so that everyone can contribute fairly to society.

To find out more, visit **www.arkfound.org**

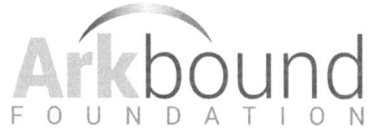

#0012 - 310718 - C0 - 203/152/6 - PB - 9781912092635